■SCHOLASTIC

BOOK *of* WORLD RECORDS 2008

by Jenifer Corr Morse

A GEORGIAN BAY BOOK

SCHOLASTIC 💡 REFERENCE

To Isabelle Nicole—May you always find wonder in the world.
–JCM

CREATED AND PRODUCED BY GEORGIAN BAY ASSOCIATES, LLC

Georgian Bay Staff
Bruce S. Glassman, Executive Editor
Jenifer Corr Morse, Photo Editor
Calico Harington, Design

Scholastic Reference Staff
Mary Varilla Jones, Senior Editor
Brenda Murray, Associate Editor
Becky Terhune, Art Director

In most cases, the graphs in this book represent the top five record holders in each category.
However, in some graphs, we have chosen to list well-known or common people, places,
animals, or things that will help you better understand how extraordinary the record holder
is. These may not be the top five in the category. Additionally, some graphs have fewer than
five entries because so few people or objects reflect the necessary criteria.

ISBN 10: 0-439-91658-5
ISBN 13: 978-0-439-91658-5

10 9 8 7 6 5 4 3 2   07 08 09 10 11
Printed in the U.S.A.   23
First printing, October 2007

CONTENTS

Popular Culture Records   166

Money and Business Records   195

Science Records   213

U.S. Records   245

Sports Records

Track and Field • Bicycling • Golf • Basketball
Baseball • Football • Tennis • Figure Skating
Skiing • Motorcycling • X-Games
Snowboarding • Soccer • Hockey • Car Racing

Runner with the
World's Fastest Mile

Hicham El Guerrouj

Runners with the
WORLD'S FASTEST MILE

Time in minutes and seconds

3:43.13	3:43.40	3:44.39	3:44.60	3:44.90
Hicham El Guerrouj, Morocco	Noah Ngeny, Kenya	Noureddine Morceli, Algeria	Hicham El Guerrouj, Morocco	Hicham El Guerrouj, Morocco

Moroccan runner Hicham El Guerrouj is super speedy—he ran a mile in just over 3 minutes and 43 seconds in July 1999 while racing in Rome. He also holds the record for the fastest mile in North America with a time just short of 3 minutes and 50 seconds. El Guerrouj is also an Olympian with gold medals in the 1500-meter and 5000-meter races. With this accomplishment at the 2004 Athens Games, he became the first runner to win both races at the same Olympics in more than 75 years. El Guerrouj returned to the Olympics in 2006 as a torchbearer in Torino, Italy.

Cyclist with the
Most Tour de France Wins

Lance Armstrong

Lance Armstrong was the first cyclist to cross the finish line to win seven Tour de France races. Armstrong won his first race in 1999, just three years after being diagnosed with cancer. He went on to win the top cycling event for the next six years, retiring after his 2005 victory. Armstrong has received many awards and honors during his career, including being named *Sports Illustrated*'s "Sportsman of the Year" in 2002. Armstrong also formed the Lance Armstrong Foundation that supports people recovering from cancer.

Cyclists with the
MOST TOUR DE FRANCE WINS

Number of first-place finishes

Lance Armstrong, USA	Eddy Merckx, Belgium	Jacques Anquetil, France	Bernard Hinault, France	Miguel Indurain, Spain
7	5	5	5	5

LPGA Golfer with the
Lowest Seasonal Average

Lorena Ochoa

Lorena Ochoa had the lowest seasonal average in the LPGA in 2006 with 69.24. In fact, that's the fourth-lowest scoring average in LPGA history! Ochoa, who entered the LPGA in 2003, accomplished several other impressive feats in 2006. She won six tournaments and was named Rolex Player of the Year. She earned almost $2.6 million, becoming just the second player to pass $2 million in earnings in a single season. During her short career, Ochoa has played in 99 LPGA events and finished in the top three 32 times.

LPGA Golfers with the
LOWEST SEASONAL AVERAGES
Seasonal average in 2006

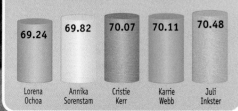

Lorena Ochoa	Annika Sorenstam	Cristie Kerr	Karrie Webb	Juli Inkster
69.24	69.82	70.07	70.11	70.48

PGA Player with the
Lowest Seasonal Average

Tiger Woods

Tiger Woods was at the top of his game in 2006 with the lowest PGA seasonal average of 68.11. Woods started his professional golfing career in 1996, and since then he has won more than 55 tournaments. Woods also helped the United States win the World Cup team title in 2000. And at 21 years old, he became the youngest person to complete the career Grand Slam of professional major championships. In 2001, he became the first golfer in history to hold all four professional major championships at the same time. Woods's career PGA winnings total more than $66.6 million.

PGA Players with the
LOWEST SEASONAL AVERAGES

Seasonal average in 2006

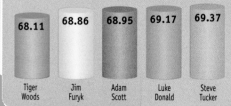

Tiger Woods	Jim Furyk	Adam Scott	Luke Donald	Steve Tucker
68.11	68.86	68.95	69.17	69.37

The LPGA's Highest-Paid Golfer

Annika Sorenstam

Annika Sorenstam has earned $20.3 million since her LPGA career began in 1994. During this time, she has had 66 career victories, including 9 majors. In 2005, Sorenstam earned her eighth Rolex Player of the Year award—the most in LPGA history. She also became the first player to sweep Rolex Player of the Year honors, the Vare Trophy, and the ADT Official Money List title five times. Sorenstam also earned her fifth consecutive Mizuno Classic title, making her the first golfer in LPGA history to win the same event five consecutive years.

The LPGA's
HIGHEST-PAID GOLFERS

Career winnings,
in millions of US dollars

Annika Sorenstam	Karrie Webb	Juli Inkster	Se Ri Pak	Meg Mallon
$20.3 M	$12.8 M	$11.3 M	$9.0 M	$8.8 M

Man with the
Most Major Tournament Wins

Jack Nicklaus

Golfing great Jack Nicklaus has won a total of 18 major championships. His wins include 6 Masters, 5 PGAs, 4 U.S. Opens, and 3 British Opens. Nicklaus was named PGA Player of the Year five times. He was a member of the winning U.S. Ryder Cup team six times and was an individual World Cup winner a record three times. He was inducted into the World Golf Hall of Fame in 1974, just 12 years after he turned professional. He joined the U.S. Senior PGA Tour in 1990. In addition to playing the game, Nicklaus has designed close to 200 golf courses and written a number of popular books about the sport.

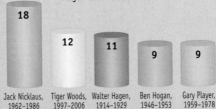

Men with the
MOST MAJOR TOURNAMENT WINS

Major tournament wins

18	12	11	9	9
Jack Nicklaus, 1962–1986	Tiger Woods, 1997–2006	Walter Hagen, 1914–1929	Ben Hogan, 1946–1953	Gary Player, 1959–1978

Women's Basketball Team with the Most NCAA Championships

Tennessee

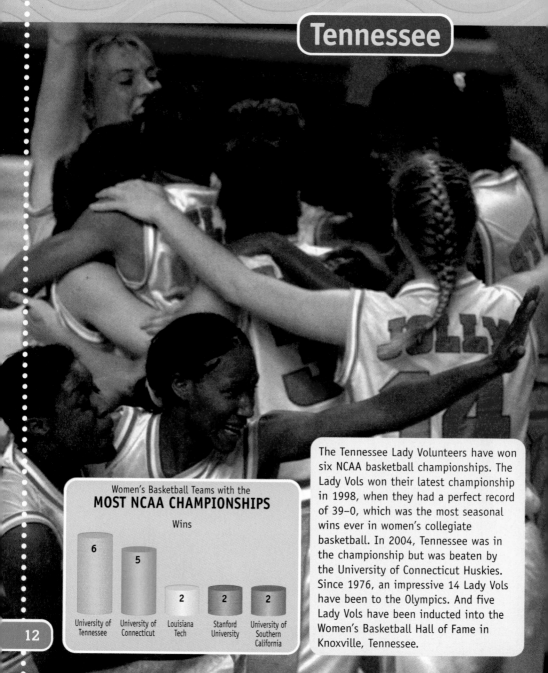

Women's Basketball Teams with the MOST NCAA CHAMPIONSHIPS

Wins

University of Tennessee	University of Connecticut	Louisiana Tech	Stanford University	University of Southern California
6	5	2	2	2

The Tennessee Lady Volunteers have won six NCAA basketball championships. The Lady Vols won their latest championship in 1998, when they had a perfect record of 39–0, which was the most seasonal wins ever in women's collegiate basketball. In 2004, Tennessee was in the championship but was beaten by the University of Connecticut Huskies. Since 1976, an impressive 14 Lady Vols have been to the Olympics. And five Lady Vols have been inducted into the Women's Basketball Hall of Fame in Knoxville, Tennessee.

Men's Basketball Team with the
Most NCAA Championships

UCLA

With 11 titles, the University of California, Los Angeles (UCLA) has the most NCAA Basketball Championship wins. The Bruins won their 11th championship in 1995. The school has won 23 of their last 41 league titles and has been in the NCAA play-offs for 35 of the last 41 years. During the final round of the NCAA championship in 2006, UCLA lost to the Florida Gators with a score of 73 to 57. Not surprisingly, UCLA has produced some basketball legends, too, including Kareem Abdul-Jabbar, Reggie Miller, and Baron Davis. For the last 36 years, the Bruins have called Pauley Pavilion home.

Men's Basketball Teams with the
MOST NCAA CHAMPIONSHIPS
Wins

UCLA	Kentucky	Indiana	North Carolina	Duke
11	7	5	4	3

NBA Team with the
Most Championship Titles

Boston Celtics

The Boston Celtics are the most successful team in the NBA with 16 championship wins. The first win came in 1957, and the team went on to win the next seven consecutive titles—the longest streak of consecutive championship wins in the history of U.S. sports. The most recent championship title came in 1986. The Celtics entered the Basketball Association of America in 1946, which later merged into the NBA in 1949. The Celtics have made the NBA play-offs for three consecutive seasons from 2001 to 2004, but they were eliminated in the first round each time.

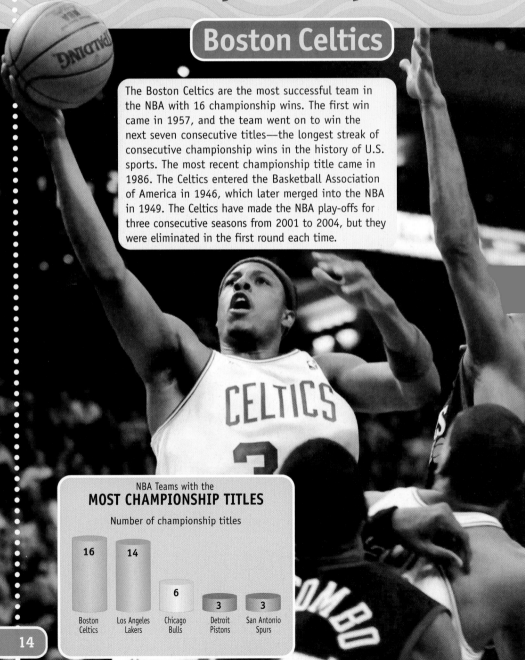

NBA Teams with the
MOST CHAMPIONSHIP TITLES

Number of championship titles

Boston Celtics	Los Angeles Lakers	Chicago Bulls	Detroit Pistons	San Antonio Spurs
16	14	6	3	3

Highest Career
Scoring Average

Wilt Chamberlain and Michael Jordan

Both Michael Jordan and Wilt Chamberlain averaged an amazing 30.1 points per game during their legendary careers. Jordan played for the Chicago Bulls and the Washington Wizards. He led the league in scoring for seven years. During the 1986 season, he became only the second person ever to score 3,000 points in a single season. Chamberlain played for the Philadelphia Warriors, the Philadelphia 76ers, and the Los Angeles Lakers. In addition to the highest scoring average, he also holds the record for the most games with 50 or more points, with 118.

Players with the
HIGHEST CAREER SCORING AVERAGES
Average points per game

30.1	30.1	28.1	27.4	27.0
Wilt Chamberlain, 1959–1973	Michael Jordan, 1984–1998; 2001–2003	Allen Iverson, 1996–	Elgin Baylor, 1958–1971	Jerry West, 1960–1974

Michael Jordan

The NBA's Highest-Scoring Team

Detroit Pistons

On December 13, 1983, the Detroit Pistons beat the Denver Nuggets with a score of 186 to 184 at McNichols Arena in Denver, Colorado. The game was tied at 145 at the end of regular play, and three overtime periods were needed to determine the winner. During the game, both the Pistons and the Nuggets each had six players who scored in the double figures. Four players scored more than 40 points each, which was an NBA first. The Pistons scored 74 field goals that night, claiming another NBA record that still stands today.

The NBA's
HIGHEST-SCORING TEAMS

Points scored by a team in one game

186	184	173	173	171
Detroit Pistons, vs. Denver Nuggets, 1983	Denver Nuggets, vs. Detroit Pistons, 1983	Boston Celtics, vs. Minneapolis Lakers, 1959	Phoenix Suns, vs. Denver Nuggets, 1990	San Antonio Spurs, vs. Milwaukee Bucks, 1982

NBA Player with the
Highest Salary

Kevin Garnett

Kevin Garnett earns $21 million a season as a forward for the Minnesota Timberwolves. Garnett—who stands 1 inch (2.5 cm) shy of 7 feet (2.1 m)— has played for the Timberwolves since he entered the NBA in 1995. Since then he has played in more than 900 games with an average of 20.5 points per game. Garnett also tops the league in rebounds, ranking number one in total rebounds (625), rebounds per game (12.5), defensive rebounds (499), and defensive rebounds per game (10).

NBA Players with the
HIGHEST SALARIES

Annual salaries, in millions of US dollars

Kevin Garnett	Allan Houston	Michael Finley	Shaquille O'Neal	Chris Webber
$21.0 M	$20.7 M	$20.2 M	$20.0 M	$18.3 M

WNBA Players with the Highest
Free Throw Scoring Average

Seimone Augustus and Eva Nemcova

WNBA Players with the
HIGHEST FREE THROW SCORING AVERAGES

Career free throw average

.897	.897	.882	.878	.871
Seimone Augustus, 2006–	Eva Nemcova, 1997–2001	Elena Tornikidou, 1999–2001	Sue Bird, 2002–	Cynthia Cooper, 1997–

Both retired player Eva Nemcova and newcomer Seimone Augustus have free throw averages of .897. Nemcova played for the Cleveland Rockets from 1997 to 2001 and was the fourth overall draft pick during the league's inaugural year. In 2000, she set a WNBA free throw record when she sank 66 consecutive shots that season. In the 2006 season, Seimone Augustus signed with the Minnesota Lynx and quickly established herself as a person not to be fouled. During her career, she has attempted 165 free throws and made 148 of them!

Seimone Augustus

Most Career
Points

Kareem Abdul-Jabbar

During his highly successful career, Kareem Abdul-Jabbar scored a total of 38,387 points. In 1969, Abdul-Jabbar began his NBA tenure with the Milwaukee Bucks. He was named Rookie of the Year in 1970. The following year he scored 2,596 points and helped the Bucks win the NBA championship. He was traded to the Los Angeles Lakers in 1975. With his new team, Abdul-Jabbar won the NBA championship in 1980, 1982, 1985, 1987, and 1988. He retired from basketball in 1989 and was inducted into the Basketball Hall of Fame in 1995.

Players with the
MOST CAREER POINTS

Points scored

Kareem Abdul-Jabbar 1969–1989	Karl Malone, 1985–2004	Michael Jordan, 1984–1998; 2001–2003	Wilt Chamberlain, 1959–1973	Moses Malone, 1974–1994
38,387	36,928	32,292	31,419	27,409

WNBA Player with the
Highest Career PPG Average

Seimone Augustus

WNBA Players with the
HIGHEST CAREER PPG AVERAGES

Average points per game*

21.9	21.0	19.5	19.5	18.6
Seimone Augustus, 2006–	Cynthia Cooper, 1997–2000	Cappie Poindexter, 2006–	Diana Taurasi, 2004–	Lauren Jackson, 1997–

*As of February 11, 2007

Minnesota Lynx Seimone Augustus leads the WNBA with an average of 21.9 points per game. Augustus was the first overall draft pick in 2006. The 6-foot- (1.8-m-) tall guard from Louisiana State was awarded the Naismith Player of the Year Award in 2005, and went on to win the AP Player of the Year Award in 2006. During her first season with the WNBA, Augustus was ranked second in points per game (21.9), field goals made (148), points (744), and field goal attempts (620).

WNBA Player with the
Most Career Points

Lisa Leslie

Lisa Leslie—center for the Los Angeles Sparks—has scored 5,412 points in her career. Leslie has a career average of 17.6 points per game. She was named MVP of the WNBA All-Star Games in 1999, 2001, and 2002. Leslie was also a member of the 1996 and 2000 Olympic gold-medal-winning women's basketball teams. In both 2001 and 2002, Leslie led her team to victory in the WNBA championship and was named Finals MVP. Leslie set another record on July 30, 2002, when she became the first player in WNBA history to slam-dunk in a game.

WNBA Players with the
MOST CAREER POINTS

Points scored*

Lisa Leslie, 1997–	Sheryl Swoopes, 1997–	Tina Thompson, 1997–	Katie Smith, 2000–	Chamique Holdsclaw, 1999–
5,412	4,376	4,243	4,127	3,896

*As of February 11, 2007

Highest Seasonal
Home-Run Total

Barry Bonds

Baseball's Top Seasonal
HOME-RUN HITTERS

Number of home runs

73	70	66	65	64
Barry Bonds, 2001	Mark McGwire, 1998	Sammy Sosa, 1998	Mark McGwire, 1999	Sammy Sosa, 2001

On October 5, 2001, Barry Bonds smashed Mark McGwire's record for seasonal home runs when he hit his 71st home run in the first inning of a game against the Los Angeles Dodgers. Two innings later, he hit number 72. Bonds, a left fielder for the San Francisco Giants, has a career total of 749 home runs. He also holds the records for seasonal walks (232) and seasonal on-base percentage (0.609). Bonds and his father, hitting coach Bobby Bonds, hold the all-time father-son home run record with 1,020.

World's All-Time
Home-Run Hitters

Hank Aaron

In 1974, Hank Aaron broke Babe Ruth's lifetime record of 714 home runs. By the time he retired from baseball in 1976, Aaron had hit a total of 755 homers—a record that has remained unbroken. His amazing hitting ability earned him the nickname "Hammerin' Hank." Aaron holds many other distinguished baseball records, including most lifetime runs batted in (2,297) and most years with 30 or more home runs (15). Aaron was an excellent defensive player, earning three Gold Glove Awards.

The World's Top 5
ALL-TIME HOME-RUN HITTERS

Home runs*

755	734	714	660	588
Hank Aaron, 1952–1976	Barry Bonds, 1986–	Babe Ruth, 1914–1935	Willie Mays, 1948–1973	Sammy Sosa, 1989–

*As of February 11, 2007

Most
Career Strikeouts

Nolan Ryan

Nolan Ryan leads Major League Baseball with an incredible 5,714 career strikeouts. In his impressive 28-year career, he played for the New York Mets, the California Angels, the Houston Astros, and the Texas Rangers. The right-handed pitcher from Refugio, Texas, led the American League in strikeouts 10 times. In 1989, at the age of 42, Ryan became the oldest pitcher ever to lead the Major Leagues in strikeouts. Ryan set another record in 1991 when he pitched his seventh career no-hitter.

Pitchers with the
MOST CAREER STRIKEOUTS

Strikeouts*

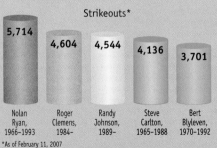

5,714	4,604	4,544	4,136	3,701
Nolan Ryan, 1966–1993	Roger Clemens, 1984–	Randy Johnson, 1989–	Steve Carlton, 1965–1988	Bert Blyleven, 1970–1992

*As of February 11, 2007

Most
Career Hits

Pete Rose

Rose belted an amazing 4,256 hits during his 23 years of professional baseball. He got his record-setting hit in 1985, when he was a player-manager for the Cincinnati Reds. By the time Pete Rose retired as a player from Major League Baseball in 1986, he had set several other career records. Rose holds the Major League records for the most career games (3,562), the most times at bat (14,053), and the most seasons with more than 200 hits (10). During his career, he played for the Cincinnati Reds, the Philadelphia Phillies, and the Montreal Expos.

Players with the
MOST CAREER HITS

Hits

4,256	4,191	3,771	3,630	3,514
Pete Rose, 1963–1986	Ty Cobb, 1905–1928	Hank Aaron, 1952–1976	Stan Musial, 1941–1963	Tris Speaker, 1907–1928

Baseball Player with the Most Expensive Contract

Alex Rodriguez

Alex Rodriguez signed a 10-year deal with the Texas Rangers for $252 million in 2001. This does not include any bonuses the shortstop may earn for winning titles or awards, or any money he could make from potential endorsements. The right-hander began his successful career with Seattle in 1994. In 2004, Rodriguez joined the New York Yankees, and the ball club is now responsible for paying the majority of his contract. In 2005, Rodriguez won the American League MVP award.

Baseball Players with the
MOST EXPENSIVE CONTRACTS

Yearly salary, in
millions of US dollars

$25.7 M	$20.6 M	$20.4 M	$20.0 M	$19.0 M
Alex Rodriguez, New York Yankees	Derek Jeter, New York Yankees	Jason Giambi, New York Yankees	Barry Bonds, San Francisco Giants	Mike Mussina, New York Yankees

MLB Player with the
Most Career Runs

Rickey Henderson

During his 25 years in the majors, baseball great Rickey Henderson boasts the most career runs with 2,295. Henderson got his start with the Oakland Athletics in 1979, and went on to play for the Yankees, the Mets, the Mariners, the Red Sox, the Padres, the Dodgers, and the Angels. Henderson won a Gold Glove Award in 1981, and the American League MVP award in 1989 and 1990. Henderson is also known as the "Man of Steal" because he holds the MLB record for most stolen bases in a career with 1,406.

MLB Players with the
MOST CAREER RUNS

Career runs

2,295	2,245	2,174	2,174	2,165
Rickey Henderson, 1979–2003	Ty Cobb, 1905–1928	Hank Aaron, 1954–1976	Babe Ruth, 1914–1935	Pete Rose, 1963–1986

Most MVP Awards in the
American League

Yogi Berra, Joe DiMaggio, Jimmie Foxx, and Mickey Mantle

With three honors each, Yogi Berra, Joe DiMaggio, Jimmie Foxx, and Mickey Mantle all hold the record for the Most Valuable Player awards during their professional careers. DiMaggio, Berra, and Mantle were all New York Yankees. Foxx played for the Athletics, the Cubs, and the Phillies. The player with the biggest gap between wins was DiMaggio, who won his first award in 1939 and his last in 1947. Also nicknamed "Joltin' Joe" and the "Yankee Clipper," DiMaggio began playing in the major leagues in 1936. The following year, he led the league in home runs and runs scored. He was elected to the Baseball Hall of Fame in 1955.

Joe DiMaggio

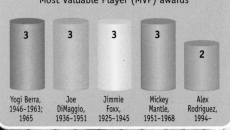

Players with the
MOST AMERICAN LEAGUE MVP AWARDS

Most Valuable Player (MVP) awards

Yogi Berra, 1946–1963; 1965	Joe DiMaggio, 1936–1951	Jimmie Foxx, 1925–1945	Mickey Mantle, 1951–1968	Alex Rodriguez, 1994–
3	3	3	3	2

Most MVP Awards in the
National League

San Francisco Giant Barry Bonds has earned seven Most Valuable Player awards for his amazing achievements in the National Baseball League. He received his first two MVP awards in 1990 and 1992 while playing for the Pittsburgh Pirates. The next five awards came while wearing the Giants uniform in 1993, 2001, 2002, 2003, and 2004. Bonds is the first player to win an MVP award three times in consecutive seasons. In fact, Bonds is the only baseball player in history to have won more than three MVP awards.

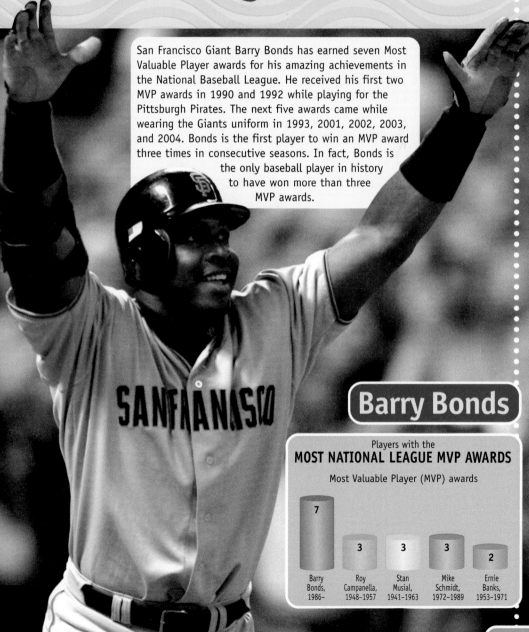

Barry Bonds

Players with the
MOST NATIONAL LEAGUE MVP AWARDS

Most Valuable Player (MVP) awards

Barry Bonds, 1986–	Roy Campanella, 1948–1957	Stan Musial, 1941–1963	Mike Schmidt, 1972–1989	Ernie Banks, 1953–1971
7	3	3	3	2

Team with the
Most World Series Wins

New York Yankees

Between 1923 and 2000, the New York Yankees were the World Series champions a record 26 times. The team picked up their latest win in October of 2000 when they beat the New York Mets. The Yankees beat the Mets four games to one to win their third consecutive championship. Since their early days, the team has included some of baseball's greatest players, including Babe Ruth, Lou Gehrig, Yogi Berra, Joe DiMaggio, and Mickey Mantle.

Teams with the
MOST WORLD SERIES WINS

Wins

NY Yankees, 1923–2000	St. Louis Cardinals, 1926–2006	Philadelphia/ Kansas City/ Oakland Athletics, 1910–1989	Brooklyn/ LA Dodgers, 1955–1988	NY/ San Francisco Giants, 1905–1954
26	10	9	6	5

Most Cy Young Awards

Roger Clemens, a starting pitcher for the Houston Astros, has earned a record seven Cy Young awards during his career so far. He set a Major League record in April 1986 when he struck out 20 batters in one game. He later tied this record in September 1996. In September 2001, Clemens became the first Major League pitcher to win 20 of his first 21 decisions in one season. In June 2003, he became the first pitcher in more than a decade to win his 300th game. He also struck out his 4,000th batter that year.

Roger Clemens

Pitchers with the
MOST CY YOUNG AWARDS

Cy Young awards

Roger Clemens, 1984–	Randy Johnson, 1988–	Steve Carlton, 1965–1988	Greg Maddux, 1986–	Sandy Koufax, 1955–1966
7	5	4	4	3

Player with the Most At Bats

Pete Rose

Pete Rose has stood behind the plate for 14,053 at bats—more than any other Major League player. Rose signed with the Cincinnati Reds after graduating high school in 1963 and played second base. During his impressive career, Rose set several other records, including the most singles in the Major Leagues (3,315), most seasons with 600 or more at bats in the major leagues (17), most career doubles in the National League (746), and most career runs in the National League (2,165). He was also named World Series MVP, *Sports Illustrated* Sportsman of the Year, and *The Sporting News* Man of the Year.

Players with the
MOST AT BATS

At bats

Pete Rose	Hank Aaron	Carl Yastrzemski	Cal Ripken, Jr.	Ty Cobb
14,053	12,364	11,988	11,551	11,429

Player with the
Most Career RBIs

Hank Aaron

During his 23 years in the major leagues, right-handed Hank Aaron batted in an incredible 2,297 runs. Aaron began his professional career with the Indianapolis Clowns, a team in the Negro American League, in 1952. He was traded to the Milwaukee Braves in 1954 and won the National League batting championship with an average of .328. He was named the league's Most Valuable Player a year later when he led his team to a World Series victory. Aaron retired as a player in 1976 and was inducted into the Baseball Hall of Fame in 1982.

Players with the
MOST CAREER RBIs

Runs batted in

2,297	2,213	2,076	1,995	1,951
Hank Aaron, 1952–1976	Babe Ruth, 1914–1935	Cap Anson, 1876–1897	Lou Gehrig, 1923–1939	Stan Musial, 1941–1963

Player Who Played the
Most Consecutive Games

Cal Ripken, Jr.

Players with the
MOST CONSECUTIVE GAMES PLAYED

Consecutive games played

Cal Ripken, Jr., 1978–2001	Lou Gehrig, 1923–1939	Everett Scott, 1914–1925	Steve Garvey, 1968–1988	Billy Williams, 1959–1974
2,632	2,130	1,307	1,207	1,117

Baltimore Oriole Cal Ripken, Jr., played 2,632 consecutive games from May 30, 1982, to September 20, 1998. The right-handed third baseman also holds the record for the most consecutive innings played: 8,243. In June 1996, Ripken also broke the world record for consecutive games with 2,216, surpassing Sachio Kinugasa of Japan. When he played as a shortstop, Ripken set Major League records for most home runs (345) and most extra base hits (855) for his position. He has started in the All-Star Game a record 19 times in a row.

Quarterback with the
Most Passing Yards

Dan Marino

Dan Marino racked up 61,361 passing yards during his 17-year career. Marino was selected by the Dolphins as the twenty-seventh pick in the first-round draft in 1983. He remained a Dolphin for the rest of his career, setting many impressive records. Marino has the most career pass attempts (8,358), the most career completions (4,967), the most career touchdown passes (420), the most passing yards in a season (5,084), and the most seasons leading the league in completions (6). Marino retired from the NFL in 2000.

Players with the
MOST PASSING YARDS
Yards

Dan Marino, 1983–2000	Brett Favre, 1991–	John Elway, 1983–1999	Warren Moon, 1984–2000	Fran Tarkenton, 1961–1978
61,361	57,500	51,475	49,325	47,003

Highest Career
Rushing Total

Emmitt Smith

Running back Emmitt Smith holds the record for all-time rushing yards with 18,355. Smith began his career with the Dallas Cowboys in 1990 and played with the team until the end of the 2002 season. In 2003, Smith signed a two-year contract with the Arizona Cardinals. Smith also holds the NFL records for the most carries with 4,142 and the most rushing touchdowns with 164. After 15 years in the NFL, Smith retired at the end of the 2004 season.

Players with the
HIGHEST CAREER RUSHING TOTALS
Rushing yards

Emmitt Smith, 1990–2004	Walter Payton, 1975–1987	Barry Sanders, 1989–1999	Curtis Martin, 1995–2007	Jerome Bettis, 1993–2006
18,355	16,726	15,269	14,101	13,662

Most Career
Touchdowns

Jerry Rice

Jerry Rice has scored a record 207 touchdowns. He is widely considered to be one of the greatest wide receivers ever to play in the National Football League. Rice holds a total of 14 NFL records, including career receptions (1,549), receiving yards (22,895), receiving touchdowns (197), consecutive 100-catch seasons (4), most games with 100 receiving yards (73), and many others. He was named NFL Player of the Year twice, *Sports Illustrated* Player of the Year four times, and NFL Offensive Player of the Year once. Rice retired from the NFL in 2005.

Players with the
MOST CAREER TOUCHDOWNS

Touchdowns scored

207	175	145	136	130
Jerry Rice, 1985–2005	Emmitt Smith, 1990–2004	Marcus Allen, 1982–1996	Marshall Faulk, 1994–2005	Cris Carter 1987–2003

Most Single-Season Touchdowns

Shaun Alexander

Players with the
MOST SINGLE-SEASON TOUCHDOWNS
Touchdowns scored

28	27	26	25	24
Shaun Alexander, 2005	Priest Holmes, 2003	Marshall Faulk, 2000	Emmitt Smith, 1995	John Riggins, 1983

Seattle Seahawks running back Shaun Alexander scored 28 touchdowns in the 2005 season. He had 27 rushing touchdowns and one receiving touchdown, and became the first player in NFL history to score 15 or more touchdowns in five consecutive seasons. He also led the league in rushing that year with 1,880 yards. For all of these achievements, Alexander was named league MVP in 2005.

During his six-year NFL career, Alexander has scored a total of 100 touchdowns and rushed for 7,817 yards.

Highest Career
Scoring Total

Gary Anderson

Gary Anderson has scored 2,434 points in his 23 seasons of professional play. In 1998, the NFL's top kicker hit 35-of-35 field goals and became the first NFL player to go an entire season without missing a kick. Anderson began his career with the Pittsburgh Steelers in 1982 and later played with the Philadelphia Eagles and the San Francisco 49ers. He joined the Vikings in 1998 and scored 542 points for them— the fifth-highest in team history. Anderson joined the Tennessee Titans in 2003 and played for two seasons before retiring.

Players with the
HIGHEST CAREER SCORING TOTALS

Points scored

Gary Anderson, 1982-2005	Morten Andersen, 1980-2004	George Blanda, 1949-1975	Norm Johnson, 1983-1999	Nick Lowery, 1978-1996
2,434	2,358	2,002	1,736	1,711

Team with the Most
Super Bowl Wins

Cowboys, 49ers, and Steelers

With five championships each, the Dallas Cowboys, the San Francisco 49ers, and the Pittsburgh Steelers all hold the record for the most Super Bowl wins. The first championship win for the Cowboys was in 1972, which was followed by wins in 1978, 1993, 1994, and 1996. Out of those 10 victories, the game with the most spectators was Super Bowl XXVII, when Dallas defeated the Buffalo Bills at the Rose Bowl in Pasadena, California, in 1993. The 49ers had their first win in 1982, and repeated their victory in 1985, 1989, 1990, and 1995.

Teams with the
MOST SUPER BOWL WINS
Super Bowls won

Dallas Cowboys	San Francisco 49ers	Pittsburgh Steelers	Green Bay Packers	Washington Redskins
5	5	5	3	3

Top-Winning NFL Coach

Don Shula

Top-Winning
NFL COACHES
Games won

347	324	270	229	209
Don Shula, 1963–1995	George Halas, 1922–1929, 1933–1941, 1946–1955, 1958–1967	Tom Landry, 1960–1988	Curly Lambeau, 1919–1957	Chuck Noel, 1969–1991

Don Shula led his teams to a remarkable 347 wins during his 33 years as a head coach in the National Football League. When Shula became head coach of the Baltimore Colts in 1963, he became the youngest head coach in football history. He stayed with the team until 1969 and reached the play-offs four times. Shula became the head coach for the Miami Dolphins in 1970 and coached them until 1995. During this time, the Dolphins reached the playoffs 20 times and won at least 10 games a season 21 times. After leading them to Super Bowl wins in 1972 and 1973, Shula became one of only five coaches to win the championship in back-to-back years.

The NFL's
Highest-Paid Player

Michael Vick

In 2005, Michael Vick signed a 10-year contract with the Atlanta Falcons worth $130 million. This included a $37 million signing bonus. The quarterback joined the Falcons in 2001 from Virginia Tech as the top overall draft pick that year. During the past six seasons, Vick has totaled more than 11,500 passing yards, and has run the ball into the end zone himself an amazing 92 times. He played in the 2002 and 2005 Pro Bowls. In 2004, he became the first quarterback to ever throw for more than 250 yards and rush for more than 100 yards in the same game. Vick has a career quarterback rating of 75.7.

The NFL's
HIGHEST-PAID FOOTBALL PLAYERS

Annual salary, in millions of US dollars

Player	Salary
Michael Vick, 2001–	$23.1 M
Matt Hasselbeck, 1999–	$19.0 M
Orlando Pace, 2000–	$18.0 M
Walter Jones, 1997–	$17.7 M
Tom Brady, 2000–	$15.6 M

NFL Team with the
Most Consecutive Games Won

New England Patriots

NFL Teams with the
MOST CONSECUTIVE GAMES WON

Consecutive games won

18	17	16	16	16
New England Patriots, 2003-2004	Chicago Bears, 1933-1934	Chicago Bears, 1941-1942	Miami Dolphins, 1971-1973	Miami Dolphins, 1983-1984

The New England Patriots won 18 consecutive games during the 2003 and 2004 seasons. After finishing September 2003 with 2 wins and 2 losses, the team went on to win the next 15 games, including Super Bowl XXXVIII. When the 2004 season began, the team continued its winning streak for the next six games. The Patriots finished the season 14-2, and went on to win Super Bowl XXXIX. With this win, the Patriots became the second team in NFL history to win three championships in four years.

43

World's Top-Earning
Female Tennis Player

Steffi Graf and Lindsey Davenport

Lindsey Davenport and Steffi Graf have each earned $21.8 million in prize money while playing in the Women's Tennis Association (WTA). Davenport turned pro in 1993 and has been the WTA's top player four times. She has won 51 WTA singles titles and 36 WTA doubles titles. Steffi Graf has scored 902 victories including 22 Grand Slam singles titles and 107 tournament titles. During her career, she was ranked number one for 377 weeks and named WTA Player of the Year seven times.

The World's Top-Earning
FEMALE TENNIS PLAYERS

Career earnings,
in millions of US dollars

$21.8 M	$21.8 M	$21.6 M	$19.5 M	$16.9 M
Steffi Graf, 1982–1999	Lindsey Davenport, 1993–	Martina Navratilova, 1975–1994	Martina Hingis, 1994–	Arantxa Sanchez-Vicario, 1988–2002

Steffi Graf

World's Top-Earning
Male Tennis Player

Pete Sampras

Pete Sampras has earned more than $43 million during his 13 years as a professional tennis player. That averages out to about $9,060 a day! In addition to being the top-earning male tennis player of all time, Sampras also holds several other titles. He has been named ATP Player of the Year a record six times, he has the most career match wins with 762, and he has been ranked number one for the most weeks with 276. Sampras also ranks fourth in all-time career singles titles with 64. Sampras retired from tennis in 2003, but returned to the game in 2006 when he signed on to play for the World Team Tennis Pro League.

The World's Top-Earning
MALE TENNIS PLAYERS

Career earnings, in millions of US dollars

$43.3 M	$31.1 M	$29.6 M	$25.1 M	$23.9 M
Pete Sampras, 1990–2003	Andre Agassi, 1986–2006	Roger Federer, 1998–	Boris Becker, 1984–1997	Yevgeny Kafelnikov, 1992–2004

Woman with the
Most Singles Grand Slam Titles

Women with the
MOST SINGLES GRAND SLAM TITLES
Titles won

24	22	19	18	18
Margaret Court Smith, 1960–1975	Steffi Graff, 1987–1999	Helen Wills-Moody, 1923–1938	Chris Evert-Lloyd, 1974–1986	Martina Navratilova, 1974–1995

Margaret Court Smith won 24 Grand Slam singles titles between 1960 and 1975. She is the only woman ever to win the French, British, U.S., and Australian titles during one year in both the singles and doubles competitions. She was only the second woman to win all four titles in the same year. During her amazing career, she won a total of 66 Grand Slam championships—more than any other woman. Court was the world's top-seeded female player from 1962 to 1965, 1969 to 1970, and 1973. She was inducted into the International Tennis Hall of Fame in 1979.

Margaret Court Smith

Man with the Most Singles
Grand Slam Titles

Pete Sampras

With 14 victories, Pete Sampras holds the record for the most Grand Slam male singles titles. He won two Australian Opens, seven Wimbledon titles, and five U.S. Opens between 1990 and 2002. After not winning a major title in two years, Sampras won a surprise victory at the 2002 U.S. Open. He was the number 17 seed and beat Andre Agassi in a three-hour final match. After a three-year retirement, Sampras began playing for the World Team Tennis Pro League in 2006.

Men with the
MOST SINGLES GRAND SLAM TITLES

Titles won

Pete Sampras, 1990–2002	Roy Emerson, 1961–1967	Bjorn Borg, 1974–1981	Rod Laver, 1960–1969	Roger Federer, 2003–
14	12	11	11	10

Top Female World-Champion Figure Skaters

Carol Heiss/ Michelle Kwan

Carol Heiss and Michelle Kwan—two of America's most successful figure skaters—have each won the Women's World Figure Skating Championships five times. Heiss, whose wins came between 1956 and 1960, also won an Olympic silver medal for women's figure skating in 1956, and then a gold medal during the 1960 Winter Olympics in Squaw Valley, California. Kwan won the World Championships in 1996, 1998, 2000, 2001, and 2003. Kwan has also won the Women's U.S. Championships a record six times. She picked up a silver medal in the 1998 Olympics and won a bronze in 2002. Kwan went to compete in the 2006 Winter Games, but she had to pull out of the competition when—after qualifying—a groin injury prevented her from continuing.

Women with the
MOST WORLD FIGURE-SKATING CHAMPIONSHIP WINS

World Championship wins

Carol Heiss, USA, 1956–1960	Michelle Kwan, USA, 1996–2003	Katarina Witt, E. Germany, 1984–1988	Sjoukje Dijkstra, Netherlands, 1962–1964	Peggy Fleming, USA, 1966–1968
5	5	4	3	3

Michelle Kwan

Top Male World-Champion
Figure Skaters

Kurt Browning, Scott Hamilton, Hayes Jenkins, and Alexei Yagudin

Alexei Yagudin

Figure skaters Kurt Browning, Scott Hamilton, Hayes Jenkins, and Alexei Yagudin have each won four world championship competitions. Yagudin is from Russia and won his World Championship titles in 1998, 2000, 2001, and 2002. In the 2001–2002 season, Yagudin became the first male skater to win a gold medal in the four major skating events—Europeans, Grand Prix Final, Worlds, and the Olympics—in the same year. Yagudin retired in 2003 due to a hip disorder. Browning is from Canada and was inducted into the Canadian Sports Hall of Fame in 1994. Hamilton and Jenkins are from the United States. Hamilton won the competitions from 1981 to 1984. He also won a gold medal in the 1984 Olympics. Jenkins's impressive skating career included winning every major championship between 1953 and 1956.

Men with the
MOST WORLD FIGURE-SKATING CHAMPIONSHIP WINS

World Championship wins

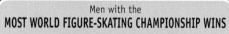

4	4	4	4	3
Kurt Browning, Canada, 1989–1993	Scott Hamilton, USA, 1981-1984	Hayes Jenkins, USA, 1953–1956	Alexei Yagudin, Russia, 1988–2002	Yevgeny Plushchenko, Russia, 2001–2004

Woman with the
Most Alpine Skiing World Cup Titles

Annemarie Moser-Proll

Austrian skier Annemarie Moser-Proll has won 17 alpine skiing world cup titles during her amazing career. Her wins include 6 in overall competition, another 7 in downhill competition, an additional 3 in giant slalom, and 1 in combined competition. Moser-Proll holds the record for World Cup Championships with 6 wins, and she also holds the record for World Cup races won with 59. Moser-Proll was also successful in Olympic competition. She won downhill and slalom silver medals in 1972, and a gold medal in the downhill in 1980.

Women with the
MOST ALPINE SKIING WORLD CUP TITLES

Total number of titles won

Annemarie Moser-Proll, Austria	Vreni Schneider, Switzerland	Katja Seizinger, Germany	Renata Gotschl, Austria	Erika Hess, Switzerland
17	14	11	10	9

Man with the
Most Alpine Skiing World Cup Titles

Ingemar Stenmark

Ingemar Stenmark is one of the most successful skiers in the world and has won 19 World Cup titles in alpine skiing. Stenmark won 3 titles in the overall competition, another 8 in the giant slalom, and 8 in the slalom. He also completed four of the top ten most successful seasons in giant slalom in history. In Olympic competition, Stenmark won a bronze medal in 1976 for giant slalom, and gold each for the slalom and giant slalom in 1980. When he retired in 1989, he had won a total of 86 World Cup races.

Men with the
MOST ALPINE SKIING WORLD CUP TITLES

Total number of titles won

Ingemar Stenmark, Sweden	Marc Girardelli, Luxembourg	Pirmin Zurbriggen, Switzerland	Hermann Maier, Austria	Phil Mahre, USA
19	15	15	14	9

Rider with the
Most Superbike Race Wins

Carl Fogarty

UK driver Carl Fogarty won 59 Superbike races during his career. Known by the nickname "Foggy" to his fans, Fogarty won the World Superbike Championship in 1994, 1995, 1998, and 1999. As part of the Ducati racing team, Fogarty set a lap record at the Island on Man TT Race after he clocked 18 minutes and 18 seconds on a Yamaha 750cc in 1992. He also competed in the 1995 Daytona 200 and finished second. Fogarty retired from racing in 2000.

Rider with the
MOST SUPERBIKE RACE WINS

Total race wins

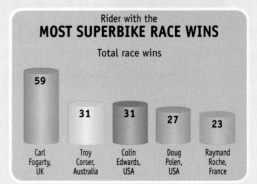

Carl Fogarty, UK	Troy Corser, Australia	Colin Edwards, USA	Doug Polen, USA	Raymand Roche, France
59	31	31	27	23

Rider with the
Most Motocross World Titles

Stefan Everts

Stefan Everts is the king of Motocross with a total of 10 World titles. He won twice on a 500cc bike, seven more times on a 250cc bike, and once on a 125cc bike. During his 18-year career, he won 101 Grand Prix victories. Everts was named Belgium Sportsman of the Year five times. He retired after his final World victory in 2006 and is a consultant and coach for the riders that compete for the KTM racing team.

Riders with the
MOST MOTOCROSS WORLD TITLES
Total FIM wins

Stefan Everts, Belgium	Joel Robert, Belgium	Roger de Coster, Belgium	Eric Geboers, Belgium	Georges Jobe, Belgium
10	6	5	5	5

Skateboarder with the
Most X-Game Gold Medals

Tony Hawk

American Tony Hawk has won 10 gold medals in the Extreme Games for skateboarding between 1995 and 2002. All his medals have come in vertical competition, meaning that the riders compete on a vert ramp similar to a half pipe. Hawk is most famous for nailing the 900—completing two and a half rotations in the air before landing back on the ramp. He has also invented many skateboarding tricks, including the McHawk, the Madonna, and the Stalefish. Although Hawk is retired from professional skateboarding, he is still active in several businesses including video game consulting, film production, and clothing design.

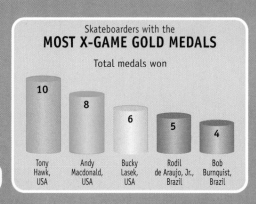

Skateboarders with the
MOST X-GAME GOLD MEDALS

Total medals won

Tony Hawk, USA	Andy Macdonald, USA	Bucky Lasek, USA	Rodil de Araujo, Jr., Brazil	Bob Burnquist, Brazil
10	8	6	5	4

Athlete with the
Most X-Game Medals

Dave Mirra

Dave Mirra has won 20 medals—14 gold, 4 silver, and 2 bronze—in X-Game competition. He has medaled in every X-Game since he entered the games in 1995. All of Mirra's medals have come in BMX competition, where he performs tricks such as double-backflips, frontflips, triple tailwhips, and backflip drop-ins. In 2006, Mirra formed his own bike company named MirraCo, and competes for the company with other top BMX riders. This same year also marked Mirra's first absence from the X-Games because of injury.

Athlete with the
MOST X-GAME MEDALS
Total medals won

Dave Mirra, USA	Tony Hawk, USA	Andy Macdonald, USA	Bob Burnquist, USA	Shaun White, USA
20	15	15	13	12

Snowboarder with the
Most Championship Medals

Nicolas Huet

Nicolas Huet has won 5 Championship medals while competing as a snowboarder with the Fédération Internationale de Ski (FIS). Huet's medals include 2 golds, 1 silver, and 2 bronzes. Huet's first medal came in 1999 when he won gold in Germany, and his most recent medals came in 2005 when he won a silver and a bronze in Canada. His medals were earned on the parallel slalom and the parallel giant slalom. Nicknamed Nico, Huet spends his time golfing and surfing when he's not on the slopes.

Snowboarders with the
MOST WORLD CHAMPIONSHIP MEDALS
Total of gold, silver, and bronze medals

Nicolas Huet, France	Jasey-Jay Anderson, Canada	Antti Autti, Finland	Mike Jacoby, USA	Helmut Pramstaller, Austria
5	3	3	3	3

Women's Soccer Team with the Most World Cup Points

USA

Women's Soccer Team with the
MOST WORLD CUP POINTS

Total World Cup points

12	8	5	3	3
USA	Germany	Sweden	China	Norway

The US Women's Soccer team has accumulated 12 points during World Cup competition. The Fédération Internationale de Football Association awards 4 points for a win, 3 points for runner up, 2 points for third place, and 1 point for fourth. The United States won the Cup in 1991 and 1999. They came in third place in 1995 and 2003. Some of the star players on the US Team at the time of these wins include Mia Hamm, Julie Foudy, Brandi Chastain, Kristine Lilly, and Briana Scurry.

Man with the Most CAPS

Mohamed Al-Deayea

Men with the MOST CAPS

Total international games played

Mohamed Al-Deayea, Saudi Arabia, 1990–2006	Claudio Suárez, Mexico, 1992–	Hossam Hassan, Egypt, 1985–	Adnan Khamées Al-Talyani, UAE, 1984–1997	Cobi Jones, United States, 1992–
181	178	170	164	164

Saudi Arabian soccer great Mohamed Al-Deayea has the most CAPS, or international games, with 181. Al-Deayea began his professional career as a goalie with the Saudi team Al-Ta'ee in 1991 and played there for 9 years. In 2000, he became a member of Al-Hilal and the team's captain. While playing as a part of the Saudi National Team, Al-Deayea reached the World Cup three times between 1994 and 2002. He was placed on the 2006 World Cup team but did not play in any games. At the end of the competition, Al-Deayea announced his retirement.

Country with the Most
World Cup Points

Germany

Germany has accumulated a total of 31 points during World Cup soccer competition. A win is worth four points, runner-up is worth three points, third place is worth two points, and fourth place is worth one point. Germany has won the World Cup four times between 1954 and 1990. Most recently, Germany earned two points for a third-place finish in 2006. The World Cup is organized by the Fédération Internationale de Football Association (FIFA) and is played every four years.

Countries with the
MOST WORLD CUP POINTS
Total points

31	30	25	14	10
Germany/ W. Germany, 1954–2006	Brazil, 1958–2002	Italy, 1934–2006	Argentina, 1978–1986	Uruguay, 1930–1950

Soccer Player with the
Highest Salary

David Beckham

Soccer Players with the
HIGHEST SALARIES

Annual salaries,
in millions of US dollars

David Beckham, Galaxy	Cristiano Ronaldo, Real Madrid	Zinédine Zidane, Real Madrid	Ronaldinho, Barcelona	Francesco Totti, AS Roma
$30.0 M	$23.0 M	$19.0 M	$14.0 M	$13.5 M

In 2006, David Beckham signed a 5-year deal with the Galaxy worth $250 million. However, only $30 million each year is for actually playing soccer— Beckham gets $10 million for competing, with an additional $20 million from Galaxy merchandise sales and participation profits. The rest of the dough comes from endorsements and advertising for such brands as Gillette, Motorola, Volkswagen, and Pepsi. Beckham had previously played for Real Madrid before coming to the United States.

Woman with the
Most CAPS

Kristine Lilly

With a total of 317, Kristine Lilly holds the world record for the most CAPS, or international games played. This is the highest number of CAPS in both the men's and women's international soccer organizations. Lilly has played more than 23,500 minutes—that's 392 hours—for the U.S. National Team. In 2004, Lilly scored her 100th international goal, becoming only one of five women to ever accomplish that. In 2005, Lilly was named U.S. Soccer's Female Athlete of the Year.

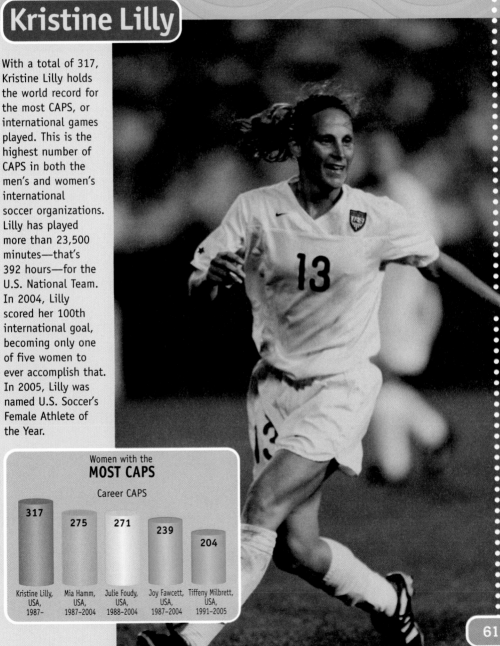

Women with the
MOST CAPS

Career CAPS

317	275	271	239	204
Kristine Lilly, USA, 1987–	Mia Hamm, USA, 1987–2004	Julie Foudy, USA, 1988–2004	Joy Fawcett, USA, 1987–2004	Tiffeny Milbrett, USA, 1991–2005

Team with the
Most Stanley Cup Wins

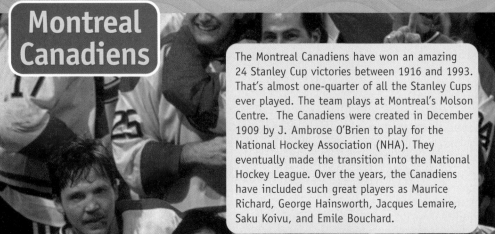

Montreal Canadiens

The Montreal Canadiens have won an amazing 24 Stanley Cup victories between 1916 and 1993. That's almost one-quarter of all the Stanley Cups ever played. The team plays at Montreal's Molson Centre. The Canadiens were created in December 1909 by J. Ambrose O'Brien to play for the National Hockey Association (NHA). They eventually made the transition into the National Hockey League. Over the years, the Canadiens have included such great players as Maurice Richard, George Hainsworth, Jacques Lemaire, Saku Koivu, and Emile Bouchard.

Team with the
MOST STANLEY CUP WINS
Stanley Cups won

Montreal Canadiens, 1916–1993	Toronto Maple Leafs, 1932–1967	Detroit Red Wings, 1936–2002	Boston Bruins, 1929–1972	Edmonton Oilers, 1984–1990
24	11	10	5	5

Montreal Canadiens with Stanley Cup

Most Career
Points

Wayne Gretzky

Wayne Gretzky scored an unbelievable 2,857 points and 894 goals during his 20-year career. Gretzky was the first person in the NHL to average more than two points per game. Many people consider Canadian-born Gretzky to be the greatest player in the history of the National Hockey League. In fact, he is called the "Great One." He officially retired from the sport in 1999 and was inducted into the Hockey Hall of Fame that same year. After his final game, the NHL retired his jersey number (99). In 2005, Gretzky became the head coach of the Phoenix Coyotes.

Players Who Scored the
MOST CAREER POINTS
Points scored

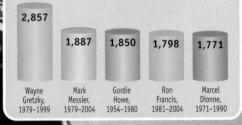

2,857	1,887	1,850	1,798	1,771
Wayne Gretzky, 1979–1999	Mark Messier, 1979–2004	Gordie Howe, 1954–1980	Ron Francis, 1981–2004	Marcel Dionne, 1971–1990

Goalie with the
Most Career Wins

Patrick Roy

During his 20 years in the NHL, Patrick Roy won 551 games. Roy also holds the NHL records for most 30-or-more win seasons (11), most playoff games played (240), most play-off minutes played (14,783), and most play-off wins (148). He was also a member of the Montreal Canadiens when they won the Stanley Cup in 1986 and 1993. Roy helped his team—the Colorado Avalanche—to win the Stanley Cup Championships in 1996 and 2001. On May 29, 2003, Roy announced his retirement from the sport.

Goaltenders with the
MOST CAREER WINS
Games won

551	480	471	447	437
Patrick Roy, 1984–2003	Martin Brodeur, 1991–	Ed Belfour, 1988–	Terry Sawchuck, 1945–1970	Jacques Plante, 1951–1975

World's Most Valuable Hockey Team

Toronto Maple Leafs

The Toronto Maple Leafs are worth an astounding $332 million, making them the most valuable hockey team in the world. This value is determined by assigning a monetary value to each of the team's players, based on their skills, performance, and contract value. Formerly known as the Toronto Arenas, the team was formed in 1917. Ten years later, the team changed to its current name. The Leafs have won 13 Stanley Cups between 1918 and 1967. Some of the most famous players associated with the team include Turk Broda, Tim Horton, Syl Apps, Darryl Sittler, and Ed Belfour. The team's home ice is at the Air Canada Centre.

The World's
MOST VALUABLE HOCKEY TEAMS

Team value,
in millions of US dollars

$332 M	$306 M	$258 M	$248 M	$246 M
Toronto Maple Leafs	New York Rangers	Detroit Red Wings	Dallas Stars	Philadelphia Flyers

Driver with the Fastest
Daytona 500 Win

Buddy Baker

Race car legend Buddy Baker dominated the competition at the 1980 Daytona 500 with a top average speed of 177 miles (285 km) per hour. It was the first Daytona 500 race run under three hours. Baker had a history of speed before this race—he became the first driver to race more than 200 miles (322 km) on a closed course in 1970. During his amazing career, Baker competed in 688 Winston Cup races—he won 19 of them and finished in the top five in 198 others. He also won more than $3.6 million. He was inducted into the International Motorsports Hall of Fame in 1997.

Drivers with the
FASTEST DAYTONA 500 WINS
Average miles/kilometers per hour

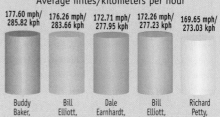

Buddy Baker, 1980	Bill Elliott, 1987	Dale Earnhardt, 1998	Bill Elliott, 1985	Richard Petty, 1981
177.60 mph/ 285.82 kph	176.26 mph/ 283.66 kph	172.71 mph/ 277.95 kph	172.26 mph/ 277.23 kph	169.65 mph/ 273.03 kph

Driver with the
Fastest Indianapolis 500 Win

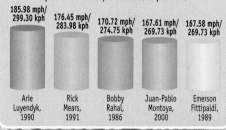

Arie Luyendyk

In 1990, race car driver Arie Luyendyk won the Indianapolis 500 with an average speed of 186 miles (299 km) per hour—the fastest average speed ever recorded in the history of the race. This was the first Indy 500 race for Luyendyk, and he drove a Lola/Chevy Indy V8 as part of the Shierson Racing team. In 1997, Luyendyk had another Indy 500 victory with an average speed of 146 miles (235 km) per hour. He also holds the record for the fastest Indy 500 practice lap at a speed of 239 miles (385 km) per hour.

Drivers with the
FASTEST INDIANAPOLIS 500 WINS
Speed in miles/kilometers per hour

185.98 mph/ 299.30 kph	176.45 mph/ 283.98 kph	170.72 mph/ 274.75 kph	167.61 mph/ 269.73 kph	167.58 mph/ 269.73 kph
Arie Luyendyk, 1990	Rick Mears, 1991	Bobby Rahal, 1986	Juan-Pablo Montoya, 2000	Emerson Fittipaldi, 1989

NASCAR Driver with the
Highest Career Earnings

Jeff Gordon

Jeff Gordon has earned more than $82 million since he began racing in 1991. In fact, he was the first driver in history to earn more than $50 million. To date, Gordon has won four Winston Cup titles, three Daytona 500 titles, and 73 NASCAR Cup victories. His first Daytona 500 win in 1997 came when he was just 25 years old, making him the race's youngest winner. Gordon has competed in more than 400 NASCAR races and finished in the top-10 almost 65% of the time. He has raced for Hendrick Motorsports since 1992, and is part owner in the business.

NASCAR Drivers with the
HIGHEST CAREER EARNINGS

Career earnings,
in millions of US dollars

Jeff Gordon	Dale Jarrett	Mark Martin	Rusty Wallace	Tony Stewart
$82.8 M	$57.1 M	$53.9 M	$49.7 M	$48.5 M

Human-Made Records

Transportation • Constructions • Travel

Country with the
Most Vehicles

United States

The Countries with the
MOST VEHICLES

Number of vehicles, in millions

216.7 M				
	73.3 M	48.0 M	37.0 M	34.6 M
USA	Japan	Germany	Italy	France

With more than 216 million vehicles registered in the United States, America outnumbers every country in the world in vehicle ownership. There are 128.7 million passenger cars and 87.9 million commercial vehicles in the country. This means that for every two Americans there is one car. That figure doesn't even include all of the trucks, campers, and motorcycles in the country. More than 90% of all U.S. residents have access to motor vehicles. With 19.1 million cars, California is the state with the most registered automobiles in the nation. The average American driver spends about 21 hours each year stuck in traffic.

City with the World's
Longest Subway System

London

The world's longest subway system runs for 244 miles (392 km) below the streets of London. The London Underground—or tube, as it's known by the locals—carries about 976 million people each year. The city's first underground railroad opened in 1863, and today it operates 500 peak trains and 275 stations. The subway's busiest station is Waterloo, which serves about 46,000 commuters during the morning rush. Throughout the subway system, some 412 escalators and 112 elevators keep commuter traffic moving.

The Cities with the World's
LONGEST SUBWAY SYSTEMS

Subway length in miles/kilometers

London	New York	Moscow	Tokyo	Paris
244 mi. 392 km.	231 mi. 372 km.	163 mi. 262 km.	160 mi. 258 km.	126 mi. 203 km.

City with the Busiest
Subway System

Tokyo

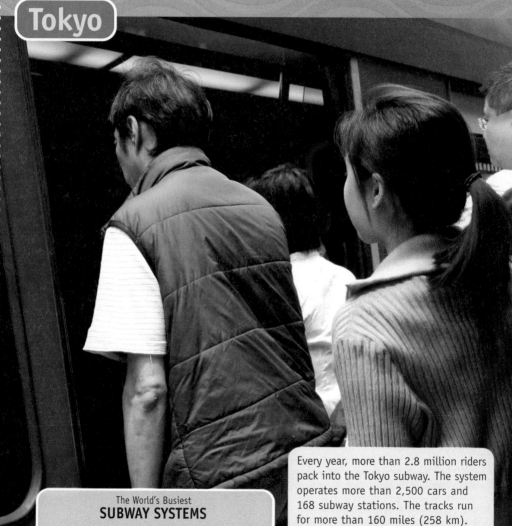

The World's Busiest
SUBWAY SYSTEMS

Passengers per year, in billions

Tokyo	Moscow	Seoul	New York City	Mexico City
2.82 B	2.60 B	2.34 B	1.45 B	1.44 B

Every year, more than 2.8 million riders pack into the Tokyo subway. The system operates more than 2,500 cars and 168 subway stations. The tracks run for more than 160 miles (258 km). The Tokyo Underground Railroad opened in 1927. It has expanded through the years to include 8 subway lines that connect the bustling areas of Chiyoda, Minato, and Chuo. The Tokyo Metro has recently taken steps to upgrade its cars and stations, reinforcing car frames and redesigning station platforms.

Country with the
Most Roads

The United States

The Countries with the
MOST ROADS

Miles/kilometers of roads

3,981,546 mi. 6,407,677 km.	2,393,173 mi. 3,851,440 km.	1,124,575 mi. 1,809,829 km.	1,071,865 mi. 1,725,000 km.	735,082 mi. 1,183,000 km.
USA	India	China	Brazil	Japan

The United States is connected by a system of roads that measures 3,981,546 miles (6,407,677 km). Approximately 2.6 million miles (4.2 million km) of these roads are paved. About three-quarters of the roads, or 2.9 million miles (4.7 million km), are part of the national road system. Americans spend about 100 hours a year driving to work. Because Americans are always on the move, it's not surprising that the nation's highways are frequently tied up with traffic jams. Americans waste about 5.7 billion hours annually because they are stuck in traffic.

73

World's Longest
Underwater Tunnel

Seikan Tunnel

At 33.4 miles (53.8 km) the Seikan Tunnel is both the longest railway tunnel and the longest underwater tunnel in the world. It connects Honshu—the main island of Japan—to Hokkaido, an island to the north. Some 14.3 miles (23 km) of the tunnel run under the Tsugaru Strait, which connects the Pacific Ocean to the Sea of Japan. A railway in the tunnel transports passengers. Construction began in 1964 and took 24 years to complete at a cost of $7 billion. Today, the Seikan Tunnel is no longer the quickest way between the two islands. Air travel is faster and almost the same price.

The World's
LONGEST UNDERWATER TUNNELS

Length in miles/kilometers

Seikan Tunnel, Japan	Channel Tunnel, France/England	Dai-Shimizu Tunnel, Japan	Shin-Kanmon Tunnel, Japan	Tokyo Bay Aqualine, Japan
33.4 mi. 53.8 km.	31.0 mi. 49.9 km.	13.8 mi. 22.2 km.	11.6 mi. 18.8 km.	5.0 mi. 9.5 km.

World's Longest Road Tunnel

Laerdal

E 16 LÆRDALSTUNNELEN
27. November 2000

The Laerdal Tunnel was officially opened in Norway on November 27, 2000, and measures 15.2 miles (24.5 km). This huge construction makes its way under large mountain chains to connect the capital, Oslo, to the port of Bergen, Norway's second-largest city. The tunnel is 29.5 feet (9 m) wide and 21 feet (6.3 m) high. It is estimated that about 1,000 cars and trucks make the 20-minute drive through the tunnel each day. To help make the tunnel safe, the designers installed special lighting to keep drivers alert. There are also turning areas in case drivers need to stop. The tunnels are equipped with state-of-the-art ventilation systems and special signal boosters that allow cell phone reception.

The World's LONGEST ROAD TUNNELS

Length in miles/kilometers

Laerdal Tunnel, Norway	St. Gotthard Tunnel, Switzerland	Arlberg Tunnel, Austria	Frejus Tunnel, France/Italy	Hsuehshan Tunnel, Taiwan
15.2 mi. 24.5 km.	10.3 mi. 16.4 km.	8.7 mi. 14.0 km.	8.0 mi. 12.9 km.	8.0 mi. 12.9 km.

World's
Highest City

Wenchuan, China

Sitting 16,730 feet (5,099 m) above the sea, Wenchuan, China, is the world's highest city. That's 3.2 miles (5.2 km) high, more than half the height of Mt. Everest. There are several ancient villages in the area with houses dating back hundreds of years. Located nearby is the Wolong Panda Preserve—one of the last places on Earth where the endangered bears are studied and bred. The city is part of the Sichuan Province, which is located in southwest China. The province covers 207,340 square miles (537,000 sq km) and has a population of 87.2 million.

The World's
HIGHEST CITIES

Height above sea level
in feet/meters

16,730 ft. 5,099 m.	13,045 ft. 3,976 m.	12,146 ft. 3,702 m.	12,087 ft. 3,684 m.	11,916 ft. 3,632 m.
Wenchuan, China	Potosi, Bolivia	Oruro, Bolivia	Lhasa, Tibet	La Paz, Bolivia

World's Longest Ship Canal

Grand Canal

The World's LONGEST SHIP CANALS

Length in miles/kilometers

Canal	Length
Grand Canal, China	1,114 mi. / 1,793 km.
Erie Canal, USA	363 mi. / 584 km.
Gota Canal, Sweden	240 mi. / 386 km.
St. Lawrence Canal, Canada/USA	180 mi. / 290 km.
Canal du Midi, France	149 mi. / 240 km.

The Grand Canal flows for 1,114 miles (1,793 km) through China, connecting Beijing to Hangzhou. The canal measures between 100 and 200 feet (30 and 60 m) wide and between 2 and 15 feet (0.6 and 4.6 m) deep. There are 24 locks and 60 bridges along the Grand Canal. Construction on the canal began in the sixth century BC and continued for 2,000 years. Since most of China's main rivers flow from west to east, the north-and-south flowing canal is an important connection between the Yangtze River valley and the Yellow River valley.

World's Largest Mall

South China Mall

The South China Mall in Dongguan City is a shopper's paradise with 7.1 million square feet (0.66 M sq m) of retail and entertainment space. There are 11 large department stores, and 1,500 smaller shops. The megamall—which opened in 2005—was designed with seven major areas that resemble Amsterdam, Paris, Rome, Venice, Egypt, the Caribbean, and California. And, for shoppers too tired to walk from one end of the giant retail outlet to the other, there are gondolas and water taxis located on the one-mile, human-made canal that circles the perimeter.

The World's LARGEST MALLS

Area in millions of square feet/square meters

South China Mall, China	Golden Resources Shopping Mall, China	West Edmonton Mall, Canada	Panda Mall, China	Grandview Mall, China
7.1 M sq. ft. 0.66 M sq. m.	6.0 M sq. ft. 0.56 M sq. m.	3.8 M sq. ft. 0.35 M sq. m.	3.2 M sq. ft. 0.30 M sq. m.	3.2 M sq. ft. 0.30 M sq. m.

Amusement Park with the Most Rides

Cedar Point

The Amusement Parks with the
MOST RIDES
Number of rides

Cedar Point, Ohio, USA	Disneyland, California, USA	HersheyPark, Pennsylvania, USA	Legoland, California, USA	Six Flags Great Adventure, New Jersey, USA
68	60	60	47	37

Located in Sandusky, Ohio, Cedar Point offers park visitors 68 rides to enjoy. Skyhawk—the park's newest ride—thrusts riders 125 feet (38 m) into the air and is the largest swing ride in the world. Top Thrill Dragster roller coaster is the tallest in the world at 420 feet (128 m). And with 16 roller coasters, Cedar Point also has the most coasters of any theme park in the world. Over 47,350 feet (14,432 m) of coaster track—more than 6 miles (9.7 km)—run through the park. Cedar Point opened in 1870 and is the second-oldest amusement park in the country.

City with the
Most Skyscrapers

Hong Kong

A total of 188 skyscrapers rise high above the streets of Hong Kong. In fact, the world's fifth-tallest building—Two International Finance Centre—towers 1,362 feet (415 m) above the city. Because this bustling Chinese business center has only about 160 square miles (414 sq km) of land suitable for building, architects have to build up instead of out. And Hong Kong keeps growing—60 of the city's giant buildings were constructed in the last seven years. Some large development projects, such as the Sky Tower Apartment Complex, added seven skyscrapers to the landscape in just one year.

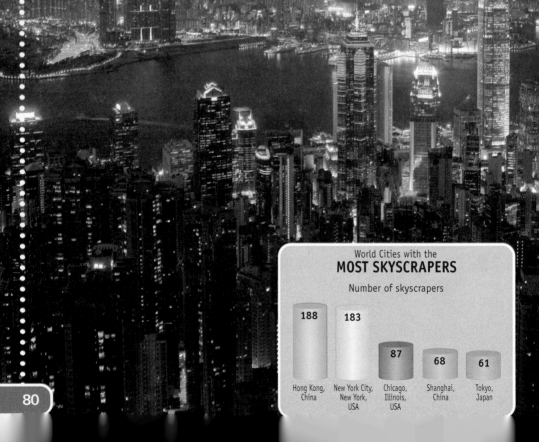

World Cities with the
MOST SKYSCRAPERS

Number of skyscrapers

Hong Kong, China	New York City, New York, USA	Chicago, Illinois, USA	Shanghai, China	Tokyo, Japan
188	183	87	68	61

World's Tallest
Apartment Building

Q1

Q1, a new luxury apartment complex on Australia's Gold Coast, rises 1,058 feet (323 m) above the surrounding sand. There are 526 apartments within the building's 80 floors. Some apartments have glass-enclosed balconies. Q1 residents can enjoy Australia's only beachside observation deck and a 10-story sky garden. Some other amenities include retail outlets, a lagoon swimming pool, spa, sauna, and fitness center. And just in case all nine elevators are out of order, there are 1,430 steps from the penthouse to the basement.

The World's
TALLEST APARTMENT BUILDINGS

Height in feet/meters

1,058 ft. 323 m.	975 ft. 297 m.	863 ft. 263 m.	656 ft. 200 m.	645 ft. 197 m.
Q1, Gold Coast, Australia	Eureka Tower, Melbourne, Australia	Trump World Towers, New York, USA	Tregunter Tower III, Hong Kong, China	Lake Point Tower, Chicago, USA

World's Largest Dome

Millennium Dome

The Millennium Dome has a roof that measures 1,050 feet (320 m) in diameter and covers 861,113 square feet (80,000 sq m). That's large enough to contain the Great Pyramid of Giza! The roof is made of 107,639 square feet (10,000 sq m) of fabric and is held up by 43 miles of steel cable. Renamed The O2, the dome will officially reopen in July 2007. It also boasts a movie complex, theaters, and restaurants. The dome was built for the country's millennium celebration. After the New Year's celebration, renovations began to turn the dome into a sports complex, and it will be used for the 2012 Olympics.

The World's
LARGEST DOMES

Dome diameter, in feet and meters

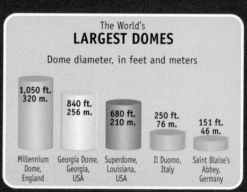

1,050 ft. 320 m.	840 ft. 256 m.	680 ft. 210 m.	250 ft. 76 m.	151 ft. 46 m.
Millennium Dome, England	Georgia Dome, Georgia, USA	Superdome, Louisiana, USA	Il Duomo, Italy	Saint Blaise's Abbey, Germany

World's Tallest Habitable Building

Taipei 101

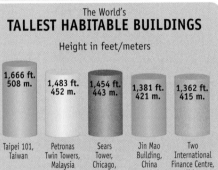

The World's TALLEST HABITABLE BUILDINGS

Height in feet/meters

1,666 ft. 508 m.	1,483 ft. 452 m.	1,454 ft. 443 m.	1,381 ft. 421 m.	1,362 ft. 415 m.
Taipei 101, Taiwan	Petronas Twin Towers, Malaysia	Sears Tower, Chicago, USA	Jin Mao Building, China	Two International Finance Centre, China

Located in Taipei's Xinyi district, Taipei 101 towers over the city at a height of 1,666 feet (508 m). To reflect Taiwan's culture, the pagoda-style office building was designed to resemble sturdy bamboo stalks growing out of the ground. The 101-story building has 2.14 million square feet (198,348 sq m) of office space, and an additional 804,182 square feet (74,711 sq m) for a shopping center. As a safety precaution, the steel-frame building was built to withstand the country's strongest earthquakes and winds at a force of 134 miles (216 km) per hour.

World's Highest
Suspension Bridge

Royal Gorge

The World's
HIGHEST SUSPENSION BRIDGES

Height in feet/meters

Royal Gorge, Colorado, USA	Viaduc de Millau, France	Tacoma Narrows, Washington, USA	Akashi-Kaikyo, Japan	Verrazano-Narrows, New York, USA
1,053 ft. 321 m.	885 ft. 270 m.	507 ft. 155 m.	318 ft. 97 m.	228 ft. 69 m.

Located in Canon City, Colorado, the Royal Gorge Bridge spans the Arkansas River 1,053 feet (321 m) above the water. The bridge is 1,260 feet (384 m) long and 18 feet (5 m) wide. About 1,000 tons (907 t) of steel make up the bridge's floor, which can hold in excess of 2 million pounds (907,200 kg). The cables weigh about 300 tons (272 t) each. The bridge took just five months to complete in 1929, at a cost of $350,000.

World's Longest
Suspension Bridge

Akashi-Kaikyo

The Akashi-Kaikyo connects Maiko, Tarumi Ward, in Kobe City, to Matsuho, Awaji Town, in Japan. Altogether, the suspension bridge spans the Akashi Strait for 2 miles (3 km) in Tsuna County on the Japanese island of Awajishima. Built in 1998, the structure's main span is a record-breaking 6,529 feet (1,990 m) long with cables supporting the 100,000-ton (90,700-t) bridge below. Each cable is made up of 290 strands of wire. The main tower soars approximately 984 feet (300 m) into the air. The bridge needed to be high above the water so it wouldn't block ships entering the Akashi Strait.

The World's
LONGEST SUSPENSION BRIDGES

Length of main span
in feet/meters

Akashi-Kaikyo, Japan	Izmit Bay, Turkey	Storebaelt, Denmark	Humber Estuary, UK	Jiangyin, China
6,529 ft. 1,990 m.	5,472 ft. 1,668 m.	5,328 ft. 1,624 m.	4,626 ft. 1,410 m.	4,544 ft. 1,385 m.

World's Most-Visited City

New York City

The World's MOST-VISITED CITIES

Annual visitors, in millions

44.0 M	37.0 M	28.0 M	26.0 M	24.5 M
New York City, USA	Tijuana, Mexico	Paris, France	San Diego, USA	London, England

In just one year, more than 44 million tourists visit New York City. That's the equivalent of the entire population of Canada coming for vacation! Both domestic and international travelers come to New York City to enjoy the theater and performing arts, museums, shopping, and historical landmarks. Collectively, visitors contribute more than $22 billion to the city's economy annually. Just more than 7 million tourists are from other countries, and most come from the United Kingdom, Canada, and Germany. During their stay, most travelers take advantage of the city's 71,000 hotel rooms and 18,696 restaurants.

World's Top
Tourist Country

France

France hosts more than 76 million tourists annually. That's more than twice the number of people living in all of New England combined. The most popular French destinations are Paris and the Mediterranean coast. In July and August—the most popular months to visit France—tourists flock to the westernmost coastal areas of the region. In the winter, visitors hit the slopes at major ski resorts in the northern Alps. Tourists also visit many of France's world-renowned landmarks and monuments, including the Eiffel Tower, Notre Dame, the Louvre, and the Arc de Triomphe. Most tourists are from other European countries, especially Germany.

The World's
TOP TOURIST COUNTRIES

International visitors, in millions

France	Spain	USA	China	Italy
76.7 M	51.7 M	41.9 M	39.8 M	36.8 M

Country with the
Most Airports

United States

There are 14,858 airports located in the United States. That is more than the number of airports for the other nine top countries combined. The top two busiest airports in the world are also located in the United States. All together, U.S. airports serve more than 660 million domestic travelers a year. With the threat of terrorism and the state of the economy, the airline industry lost $10 billion in 2002. In September 2005, rising fuel costs and competition from discount airlines caused several major airlines—including Delta and Northwest— to file for bankruptcy. Since then, overall airline traffic has increased about 4%.

The Countries with the
MOST AIRPORTS

Number of airports

USA	Brazil	Mexico	Russia	Argentina
14,858	4,276	1,839	1,623	1,381

World's
Busiest Airport

The Hartsfield-Jackson Atlanta International Airport served almost 86 million travelers in one year. That's more people than are living in California, Texas, and Florida combined. Approximately 2,600 planes depart and arrive at this airport every day. With parking lots, runways, maintenance facilities, and other buildings, the Hartsfield terminal complex covers about 130 acres (53 ha). Hartsfield-Jackson Atlanta International Airport has a north and a south terminal, as well as an underground train, and six concourses that feature many shops, restaurants, and banks.

Hartsfield - Jackson Atlanta International Airport

The World's
BUSIEST AIRPORTS

Annual passengers, in millions

85.9 M	75.5 M	67.9 M	63.3 M	61.5 M
Hartsfield-Jackson Atlanta Intl., USA	Chicago O'Hare Intl., USA	Heathrow Intl., England	Haneda Intl., Japan	Los Angeles Intl., USA

United States' Most-Visited National Site

Blue Ridge Parkway

The United States' MOST-VISITED NATIONAL SITES

Annual visitors, in millions

17.88 M	13.60 M	9.19 M	8.29 M	7.69 M
Blue Ridge Parkway, North Carolina–Virginia	Golden Gate National Recreation Area, California	Great Smoky Mountains, Tennessee–North Carolina	Gateway National Recreation Area, New Jersey–New York	Lake Mead National Recreation Area, Arizona–Nevada

Each year nearly 18 million people travel to North Carolina and Virginia to visit the Blue Ridge Parkway. The Blue Ridge is part of the eastern Appalachian Mountains and has an average elevation of 3,000 feet (914 m). The 469-mile (755 km) stretch of road winds through four national forests. Construction began on the country's first scenic parkway in 1935, and was completed in 1987. Some of the most popular activities along the Blue Ridge Parkway include hiking, camping, bicycling, and photographing nature.

Nature Records

Animals • Natural Formations
Food • Weather • Plants • Disasters

World's Largest Crustacean

Giant Spider Crab

The giant spider crab has a 12-foot- (3.7-m-) wide leg span. That's almost wide enough to take up two parking spaces! The crab's body measures about 15 inches (38.1 cm) wide. Its ten long legs are jointed, and the first set has large claws at the end. The giant sea creature can weigh between 35 and 44 pounds (16 and 20 kg). It feeds on dead animals and shellfish it finds on the ocean floor. Giant spider crabs live in the deep water of the Pacific Ocean off southern Japan.

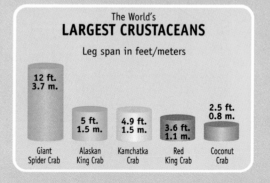

The World's
LARGEST CRUSTACEANS

Leg span in feet/meters

12 ft. 3.7 m.	5 ft. 1.5 m.	4.9 ft. 1.5 m.	3.6 ft. 1.1 m.	2.5 ft. 0.8 m.
Giant Spider Crab	Alaskan King Crab	Kamchatka Crab	Red King Crab	Coconut Crab

World's Loudest Animal

Blue Whale

The World's LOUDEST ANIMALS

In decibels

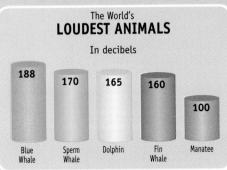

Blue Whale	Sperm Whale	Dolphin	Fin Whale	Manatee
188	170	165	160	100

The loudest animal on Earth is the blue whale. The giant mammal's call can reach up to 188 decibels—about 40 decibels louder than a jet engine. The rumbling, low-frequency sounds of the blue whale can travel several miles underwater. The whale's whistling call can be heard for several hundred miles below the sea. Much of this whale chatter is used for communication, especially during the mating season. People cannot detect the whales' calls, however, because they are too low-pitched for humans' ears.

World's
Biggest Fish

Whale Shark

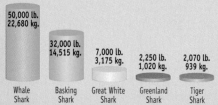

The World's
BIGGEST FISH

Average weight in pounds/kilograms

50,000 lb. 22,680 kg.	32,000 lb. 14,515 kg.	7,000 lb. 3,175 kg.	2,250 lb. 1,020 kg.	2,070 lb. 939 kg.
Whale Shark	Basking Shark	Great White Shark	Greenland Shark	Tiger Shark

Although the average length of a whale shark is 30 feet (9 m), many have been known to reach up to 60 feet (18 m) long. That's the same length as two school buses! Whale sharks also weigh an average of 50,000 pounds (22,680 kg). As with most sharks, the females are larger than the males. Their mouths measure about 5 feet (1.5 m) long and contain about 3,000 teeth. Amazingly, these gigantic fish eat only microscopic plankton and tiny fish. They float near the surface looking for food.

World's Largest Pinniped

Southern Elephant Seal

The World's LARGEST PINNIPEDS

Length in feet/meters

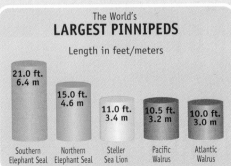

Southern Elephant Seal	Northern Elephant Seal	Steller Sea Lion	Pacific Walrus	Atlantic Walrus
21.0 ft. 6.4 m	15.0 ft. 4.6 m	11.0 ft. 3.4 m	10.5 ft. 3.2 m	10.0 ft. 3.0 m

The southern elephant seal is the largest member of the seal and sea lion family (or pinnipeds), with bulls (males) measuring more than 21 feet (6.4 m) long and weighing up to 8,800 pounds (3,992 kg). This giant pinniped got its name from its long nose that resembles an elephant's trunk. Southern elephant seals are also amazing divers and can reach depths of 3,280 feet (1,000 m) for up to 2 hours. These smart animals are very social and live in large groups. Their largest colonies are found around South Georgia and Macquarie Island.

World's
Slowest Fish

Sea Horse

With a speed of just .001 miles (.002 km) per hour, sea horses don't get anywhere fast. At that rate of speed, it would take the fish about an hour to swim only 5 feet (1.5 m). They range in size from less than half an inch (1 cm) to almost 1 foot (0.3 m). Sea horses spend most of their time near the shore. There, they can hold on to plants with their tails. This helps them avoid enemies. Approximately 50 different species of sea horses are found throughout the world. However, due to overharvesting, the sea horse population has decreased by up to 95%.

Some of the World's
SLOWEST FISH

Average speed in miles/kilometers

Sea Horse	Barracuda	Tiger Shark	Tarpon	Swordfish
.001 mph .002 kph	25 mph 40 kph	33 mph 53 kph	35 mph 56 kph	40 mph 64 kph

World's Fastest Fish

Sailfish

The World's
FASTEST FISH

Recorded speed in miles/kilometers per hour

Sailfish	Marlin	Bluefin Tuna	Yellowfin Tuna	Blue Shark
69 mph 109 kph	50 mph 80 kph	46 mph 74 kph	44 mph 70 kph	43 mph 69 kph

A sailfish once grabbed a fishing line and dragged it 300 feet (91 m) away in just 3 seconds. That means it was swimming at an average speed of 69 miles (109 km) per hour—just higher than the average speed limit on the highway! Sailfish are very large—they average 6 feet (1.8 m) long, but can grow up to 11 feet (3.4 m). Sailfish eat squid and surface-dwelling fish. Sometimes several sailfish will work together to catch their prey. They are found in both the Atlantic and Pacific oceans and prefer a water temperature of about 80°F (27°C).

World's Largest Bird Wingspan

Marabou Stork

With a wingspan that can reach up to 13 feet (4 m), the Marabou stork has the largest wingspan of any bird. These large storks weigh up to 20 pounds (9 kg) and can grow up to 5 feet (150 cm) tall. Their long leg and toe bones are actually hollow. This adaptation is very important for flight because it makes the bird lighter. Although marabous eat insects, small mammals, and fish, the majority of their food is carrion—already-dead meat. In fact, the stork's head and neck do not have any feathers. This helps the bird stay clean as it sticks its head into carcasses to pick out scraps of food.

The World's LARGEST BIRD WINGSPANS

Wingspan in feet/meters

Marabou Stork	Albatross	Trumpeter Swan	Mute Swan	Whooper Swan
13 ft. 4 m.	12 ft. 3.7 m.	11 ft. 3.4 m.	10 ft. 3 m.	10 ft. 3 m.

World's Fastest Flyer

Peregrine Falcon

A peregrine falcon can reach speeds of up to 175 miles (282 km) an hour while diving through the air. That's about the same speed as the fastest race car in the Indianapolis 500. These powerful birds can catch prey in midair and kill it instantly with their sharp claws. Peregrine falcons range from about 13 to 19 inches (33 to 48 cm) long. The female is called a falcon, but the male is called a tercel, which means "one-third" in German. This is because the male is about one-third the size of the female.

The World's
FASTEST FLYERS

Top speed in miles/kilometers per hour

Peregrine Falcon	Spine-tailed Swift	Frigate Bird	Spur-winged Goose	Red-breasted Merganser
175 mph 282 kph	106 mph 171 kph	95 mph 153 kph	88 mph 142 kph	80 mph 129 kph

World's Longest Bird Migration

Arctic Tern

The World's
LONGEST BIRD MIGRATIONS

Round-trip migration in miles/kilometers

22,000 mi. 35,406 km.	20,000 mi. 32,187 km.	20,000 mi. 32,187 km.	18,000 mi. 28,968 km.	15,000 mi. 24,140 km.
Arctic Tern	White-rumped Sandpiper	Red Knot	Lesser Yellowleg	Swainson's Hawk

The arctic tern migrates from Maine to the coast of Africa, and then on to Antarctica, flying some 22,000 miles (35,406 km) a year. That's almost the same measurement as the Earth's circumference. Some don't complete the journey however—young terns fly the first half of the journey with parents, but remain in Antarctica for a year or two. When they have matured, the birds fly back to Maine and the surrounding areas. Scientists are puzzled by how these birds remember the way back after only making the journey once so early in their lives.

Bird That Builds the Largest Nest

Bald Eagle

The World's
LARGEST BIRDS' NESTS

Diameter in feet/meters

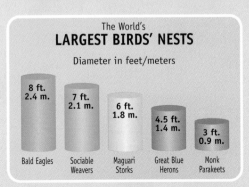

8 ft. 2.4 m.	7 ft. 2.1 m.	6 ft. 1.8 m.	4.5 ft. 1.4 m.	3 ft. 0.9 m.
Bald Eagles	Sociable Weavers	Maguari Storks	Great Blue Herons	Monk Parakeets

With a nest that can measure 8 feet (2.4 m) wide and 16 feet (4.9 m) deep, bald eagles have plently of room to move around. These birds of prey have wingspans of up to 7.5 feet (2.3 m) and need a home that they can nest in comfortably. By carefully constructing their nest with sticks, branches, and plant material, a pair of bald eagles can balance their home—which can weigh up to 4,000 pounds (8,800 kg)—on the top of a tree or cliff. These nests are usually located by rivers or coastlines, the birds' watery hunting grounds. Called an aerie, this home will be used for the rest of the eagles' lives.

World's Largest Bird Egg

Ostrich Egg

Ostriches—the world's largest birds—can lay eggs that measure 5 inches by 6 inches (13 cm by 16 cm) and weigh up to 4 pounds (1.8 kg). In fact, just one ostrich egg equals up to 24 chicken eggs. The egg yolk makes up one-third of the volume. Although the egg shell is only .08 inch (2 mm) thick, it is tough enough to withstand the weight of a 345-pound (157-kg) ostrich. A hen ostrich can lay from 10 to 70 eggs each year. Females are usually able to recognize their own eggs, even when they are mixed in with those of other females in their shared nest.

The World's LARGEST BIRD EGGS

Weight of egg in pounds/kilograms

Ostrich	Emu	Kiwi	Emperor Penguin	Albatross
4.0 lb. 1.8 kg.	1.8 lb. 0.82 kg.	1.6 lb. 0.72 kg.	1.5 lb. 0.68 kg.	1.0 lb. 0.45 kg.

World's Fastest Land Bird

Ostrich

An ostrich can run at a top speed of 45 miles (72.4 km) per hour for about 30 minutes. This allows the speedy bird to easily outrun most predators. Its long, powerful legs help an ostrich cover 10 to 15 feet (3.1 to 4.6 km) per bound. And although it is a flightless bird, an ostrich uses it wings for balance when it runs. If an ostrich does need to defend itself, it has a kick powerful enough to kill a lion. The ostrich, which is also the world's largest bird at 10 feet (3.1 m) tall and 350 pounds (158.8 kg), is native to the savannas of Africa.

The World's
FASTEST LAND BIRDS

Speed in miles/kilometers per hour

Ostrich	Emu	Wild Turkey	Roadrunner	Yellow-billed Cuckoo
45 mph 72.4 kph	40 mph 64.4 kph	20 mph 32.2 kph	17 mph 27.4 kph	15 mph 24.1 kph

World's Fastest Shark

Mako Shark

A mako shark can cruise through the water at 50 miles (79.4 km) per hour—about the speed limit of most highways. This super speed helps the shark catch its food, which consists mostly of tuna, herring, mackerel, swordfish, and porpoise. Occasionally makos even build up enough speed to leap out of the water. Mako sharks average 7 feet (2.1 m) in length, but can grow up to 12 feet (3.7 m) and weigh 1,000 pounds (454 kg). The sharks are found in temperate and tropical seas throughout the world.

The World's FASTEST SHARKS

Fastest speed in miles/kilometers per hour

Mako Shark	Blue Shark	Great White Shark	Tiger Shark	Lemon Shark
50 mph 79.4 kph	43 mph 69.2 kph	25 mph 40.2 kph	22 mph 35.4 kph	20 mph 32.2 kph

World's Heaviest
Marine Mammal

Blue Whale

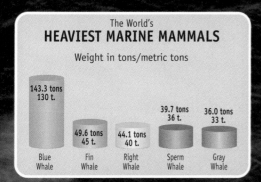

The World's
HEAVIEST MARINE MAMMALS

Weight in tons/metric tons

143.3 tons
130 t.

49.6 tons
45 t.

44.1 tons
40 t.

39.7 tons
36 t.

36.0 tons
33 t.

| Blue Whale | Fin Whale | Right Whale | Sperm Whale | Gray Whale |

Blue whales are the largest animals that have ever inhabited earth. They can weigh more than 143.3 tons (130 t) and measure over 100 feet (30 m) long. Amazingly, these gentle giants only eat krill—small, shrimplike animals. A blue whale can eat about 4 tons (3.6 t) of krill each day in the summer, when food is plentiful. To catch the krill, a whale gulps as much as 17,000 gallons (64,600 l) of seawater into its mouth at one time. Then it uses its tongue—which can be the same size as a car—to push the water back out. The krill get caught in hairs on the whale's baleen (a keratin structure that hangs down from the roof of the whale's mouth).

World's Heaviest Land Mammal

African Elephant

Weighing in at up to 14,430 pounds (6,545 kg) and measuring approximately 24 feet (7.3 m) long, African elephants are truly humongous. Even at their great size, they are strictly vegetarian. They will, however, eat up to 500 pounds (226 kg) of vegetation a day! Their two tusks—which are really elongated teeth—grow continuously during their lives and can reach about 9 feet (2.7 m) in length. Elephants live in small groups of 8 to 15 family members with one female (called a cow) as the leader.

The World's HEAVIEST LAND MAMMALS

In pounds/kilograms

African Elephant	White Rhinoceros	Hippopotamus	Giraffe	American Bison
14,430 lb. 6,545 kg.	7,937 lb. 3,600 kg.	5,512 lb. 2,300 kg.	3,527 lb. 1,600 kg.	2,205 lb. 1,000 kg.

World's
Largest Rodent
Capybara

The World's
LARGEST RODENTS
Weight in pounds/kilograms

Capybara	Porcupine	Pacarana	Patagonian Cavy	Plains Viscacha
75–150 lb. 34–68 kg.	40–57 lb. 18–26 kg.	22–33 lb. 10–15 kg.	21–33 lb. 10–15 kg.	16-20 lb. 7-8 kg.

Capybaras reach an average length of 4 feet (1.2 m), stand about 20 inches (51 cm) tall, and weigh between 75 and 150 pounds (34 to 68 kg)! That's about the same size as a Labrador retriever. Also known as water hogs and carpinchos, capybaras are found in South and Central America, where they spend much of their time in groups looking for food. They are strictly vegetarian and have been known to raid gardens for melons and squash. Their partially webbed feet make capybaras excellent swimmers. They can dive down to the bottom of a lake or river to find plants and stay there for up to five minutes.

World's
Slowest Land Mammal

Three-toed Sloth

A three-toed sloth can reach a top speed of only .07 miles (.11 km) per hour while traveling on the ground. That means that it would take the animal almost 15 minutes to cross a four-lane street. The main reason sloths move so slowly is that they cannot walk like other mammals. They must pull themselves along the ground using only their sharp claws. Because of this, sloths spend the majority of their time in trees. There, they will sleep up to 18 hours each day. When they wake at night, they search for leaves and shoots to eat.

Some of the World's
SLOWEST LAND MAMMALS

Maximum speed in miles/kilometers per hour

Three-toed Sloth	Koala	Gibbon	Pig	Squirrel
.07 mph .11 kph	7 mph 11.3 kph	10 mph 16.1 kph	11 mph 18 kph	12 mph 19 kph

World's
Fastest Land Mammal

Cheetah

The World's
FASTEST LAND MAMMALS

Maximum speed in
miles/kilometers per hour

Cheetah	Pronghorn Antelope	Mongolian Gazelle	Springbok	Grant's Gazelle/ Thompson's Gazelle
65 mph 105 kph	55 mph 89 kph	50 mph 80 kph	50 mph 80 kph	47 mph 76 kph

For short spurts these sleek mammals can reach a speed of 65 miles (105 km) per hour. They can accelerate from 0 to 40 miles (64 km) per hour in just three strides. Their quickness easily enables these large African cats to outrun their prey. All other African cats must stalk their prey because they lack the cheetah's amazing speed. Unlike the paws of all other cats, cheetah paws do not have skin sheaths (thin protective coverings). Their claws, therefore, cannot pull back.

World's Tallest Land Animal

Giraffe

Giraffes are the giants among mammals, growing to more than 18 feet (5.5 m) in height. That means an average giraffe could look through the window of a two-story building. A giraffe's neck is 18 times longer than a human's, but both mammals have exactly the same number of neck bones. A giraffe's long legs enable it to outrun most of its enemies. When cornered, a giraffe has been known to kill a lion with a single kick.

Some of the World's
TALLEST ANIMALS

Height in feet/meters

18 ft. 5.5 m.	7 ft. 2 m.	6.5 ft. 2 m.	6 ft. 1.8 m.	5 ft. 1.5 m.
Giraffe	African Elephant	Camel	Moose	Rhino

World's Largest Bat

Giant Flying Fox

A giant flying fox—a member of the megabat family—can have a wingspan of up to 6 feet (2 m). These furry mammals average just 7 wing beats per second, but can travel more than 40 miles (64 km) a night in search of food. Unlike smaller bats, flying foxes rely on their acute vision and sense of smell to locate fruit, pollen, and nectar. Flying foxes got their name because their faces resemble a fox's face. Megabats live in the tropical areas of Africa, Asia, and Australia.

The World's
LARGEST BATS

Wingspan in feet/meters

6.0 ft. 1.8 m.	5.7 ft. 1.7 m.	5.5 ft. 1.7 m.	5.0 ft. 1.5 m.	4.4 ft. 1.3 m.
Giant Flying Fox	Malayan Flying Fox	Golden Crown	Lyle's Flying Fox	Indian Flying Fox

World's Most
Deadly Amphibian

Poison Dart Frog

Poison dart frogs are found mostly in the tropical rain forests of Central and South America, where they live on the moist land. These lethal amphibians have enough poison to kill up to 20 adults. A dart frog's poison is so effective that native Central and South Americans sometimes coat their hunting arrows or hunting darts with it. These brightly colored frogs can be yellow, orange, red, green, blue, or any combination of these colors and measure only .5 to 2 inches (1 to 5 cm) long. There are approximately 75 different species of poison dart frogs.

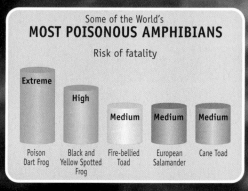

Some of the World's
MOST POISONOUS AMPHIBIANS

Risk of fatality

Extreme	High	Medium	Medium	Medium
Poison Dart Frog	Black and Yellow Spotted Frog	Fire-bellied Toad	European Salamander	Cane Toad

World's Longest Snake

Reticulated Python

Some adult reticulated pythons can grow to 27 feet (8.2 m) long, but most reach an average length of 17 feet (5 m). That's almost the length of an average school bus. These pythons live mostly in Asia, from Myanmar to Indonesia to the Philippines. The python has teeth that curve backward and can hold the snake's prey still. It hunts mainly at night and will eat mammals and birds. Reticulated pythons are slow-moving creatures that kill their prey by constriction, or strangulation.

The World's LONGEST SNAKES

Length in feet/meters

Reticulated Python	Anaconda	Rock Python	King Cobra	Oriental Rat Snake
27.0 ft. 8.2 m.	25.0 ft. 7.6 m.	24.6 ft. 7.5 m.	17.7 ft. 5.4 m.	12.2 ft. 3.7 m.

Snake with the
Longest Fangs

Gaboon Viper

The fangs of a Gaboon viper measure 2 inches (5 cm) in length! These giant fangs fold up against the snake's mouth so it does not pierce its own skin. When it is ready to strike its prey, the fangs snap down into position. The snake can grow up to 7 feet (2 m) long and weigh 18 pounds (8 kg). It is found in Africa and is perfectly camouflaged for hunting on the ground beneath leaves and grasses. The Gaboon viper's poison is not as toxic as some other snakes, but it is quite dangerous because of the amount of poison it can inject at one time. The snake is not very aggressive, however, and usually only attacks when bothered.

Snakes with the
LONGEST FANGS

Fang length in inches/centimeters

2.0 in. 5.1 cm.	1.5 in. 3.8 cm.	1.0 in. 2.5 cm.	1.0 in. 2.5 cm.	0.7 in. 1.8 cm.
Gaboon Viper	Bushmaster	Black Mamba	Diamondback Rattlesnake	Australian Taipan

World's
Deadliest Snake

Black Mamba

The World's
DEADLIEST SNAKES

Deaths possible per bite

Black Mamba	Taipan	Russell's Viper	Common Krait	Forest Cobra
200	170	150	60	50

With just one bite, an African black mamba snake releases a venom powerful enough to kill up to 200 humans. A bite from this snake is almost always fatal if it is not treated immediately. This large member of the cobra family grows to about 14 feet (4.3 m) long. In addition to its deadly poison, it is also a very aggressive snake. It will raise its body off the ground when it feels threatened. It then spreads its hood and strikes swiftly at its prey with its long front teeth. A black mamba is also very fast—it can move along at about 7 miles (11.7 km) per hour for short bursts.

World's Largest Amphibian

Chinese Giant Salamander

The World's LARGEST AMPHIBIANS

Size in feet/meters

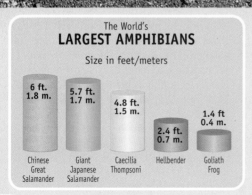

6 ft. 1.8 m.	5.7 ft. 1.7 m.	4.8 ft. 1.5 m.	2.4 ft. 0.7 m.	1.4 ft 0.4 m.
Chinese Great Salamander	Giant Japanese Salamander	Caecilia Thompsoni	Hellbender	Goliath Frog

With a length of 6 feet (1.8 m) and a weight of 55 pounds (25 kg), Chinese giant salamanders rule the amphibian world. This amphibian has a large head, but its eyes and nostrils are small. It has short legs, a long tail, and very smooth skin. This large amphibian can be found in the streams of northeastern, central, and southern China. It feeds on fish, frogs, crabs, and snakes. The giant Chinese salamander will not hunt its prey. It will wait until a potential meal wanders too close and then grab it in its mouth. Because many people enjoy the taste of the salamander's meat, it is often hunted and its population is shrinking.

World's Longest-Lived
Reptile

Galápagos Tortoise

The World's
LONGEST-LIVED REPTILES

Maximum age in years

Galápagos Tortoise	Box Turtle	American Alligator	Boa Constrictor	Komodo Dragon
150	120	50	30	20

Some Galápagos tortoises have been known to live to the old age of 150 years. Galápagos tortoises are also some of the largest tortoises in the world, weighing in at up to 500 pounds (226 kg). Even at their great size, these creatures can pull their heads, tails, and legs completely inside their shells. Amazingly, Galápagos tortoises can go without eating or drinking for many weeks. Approximately 10,000 of these tortoises live on the Galapagos island chain west of Ecuador.

World's Largest Lizard

Komodo Dragon

The World's
LARGEST LIZARDS

Length in feet/meters

Komodo Dragon	Water Monitor	Perenty	Common Iguana	Marine Iguana
10.0 ft. 3.0 m.	8.8 ft. 2.7 m.	7.8 ft. 2.4 m.	5.0 ft. 1.5 m.	5.0 ft. 1.5 m.

With a length of 10 feet (3 m) and a weight of 300 pounds (136 kg), Komodo dragons are the largest lizards roaming the Earth. A Komodo dragon has a long neck and tail, and strong legs. These members of the monitor family are found mainly on Komodo Island, located in the Lesser Sunda Islands of Indonesia. Komodos are dangerous and have even been known to attack and kill humans. A Komodo uses its sense of smell to locate food. It uses its long, yellow tongue to pick up an animal's scent. A Komodo can consume 80% of its body weight in just one meal!

World's Largest Reptile

Saltwater Crocodile

Saltwater crocodiles can grow to more than 22 feet (6.7 m) long. That's about twice the length of the average car. However, males usually measure only about 17 feet (5 m) long, and females normally reach about 10 feet (3 m) in length. A large adult will feed on buffalo, monkeys, cattle, wild boar, and other large mammals. Saltwater crocodiles are found throughout the East Indies and Australia. Despite their name, saltwater crocodiles can also be found in freshwater and swamps. Some other common names for this species are the estuary crocodile and the Indo-Pacific crocodile.

The World's
LARGEST REPTILES

Maximum length in feet/meters

Saltwater Crocodile	Gharial	Black Caiman	Orinoco Crocodile	American Alligator
22 ft. 6.7 m.	21 ft. 6.4 m.	20 ft. 6.2 m.	20 ft. 6.1 m.	13 ft. 3.9 m.

World's
Largest Spider

Goliath Birdeater

A Goliath birdeater is about the same size as a dinner plate—it can grow to a total length of 11 inches (28 cm) and weigh about 6 ounces (170 g). A Goliath's spiderlings are also big—they can have a 6-inch (15-cm) leg span after just one year. These giant tarantulas are found mostly in the rain forests of Guyana, Suriname, Brazil, and Venezuela. The Goliath birdeater's name is misleading—they commonly eat insects and small reptiles. Similar to other tarantula species, the Goliath birdeater lives in a burrow. The spider will wait by the opening to ambush prey that gets too close.

The World's
LARGEST SPIDERS

Length in inches/centimeters

Goliath Birdeater	Salmon Pink Birdeater	Slate Red Ornamental	King Baboon	Colombian Giant Redleg
11 in. 28 cm.	10.5 in. 27 cm.	9 in. 23 cm.	8 in. 20 cm.	8 in. 20 cm.

World's Fastest-Flying Insect

Hawk Moth

The average hawk moth—which got its name from its swift and steady flight—can cruise along at speeds of up to 33 miles (53 km) per hour. That's faster than the average speed limit on most city streets. Although they are found throughout the world, most species live in tropical climates. Also known as the sphinx moth and the hummingbird moth, this large insect can have a wingspan that reaches up to 8 inches (20 cm). The insect also has a good memory and may return to the same flowers at the same time each day.

The World's FASTEST-FLYING INSECTS

Speed in miles/kilometers per hour

33.3 mph
53.6 kph
Hawk Moth

30.0 mph
48.2 kph
West Indian Butterfly

30.0 mph
48.2 kph
Deer Botfly

17.8 mph
28.6 kph
Dragonfly

13.3 mph
21.4 kph
Hornet

World's Fastest-Running Insect

Australian Tiger Beetle

Australian tiger beetles can zip along at about 5.7 miles (9.2 km) per hour—that's about 170 body lengths per second! If a human could run at the same pace, he or she would run about 340 miles (547.2 km) per hour. Australian tiger beetles use their terrific speed to run down prey. Once a meal has been caught, the beetle chews it up in its powerful jaws and coats it in digestive juice. When the prey has become soft, the tiger beetle rolls it together and eats. These fierce beetles, which got their name from their skillful hunting, will also bite humans when provoked.

The World's
FASTEST-RUNNING INSECTS
Speed in miles/kilometers per hour

5.7 mph
9.2 kph
Australian
Tiger Beetle

3.5 mph
5.6 kph
American
Cockroach

1.2 mph
1.9 kph
Centipede

1.0 mph
1.6 kph
Ant

0.8 mph
1.3 kph
Mother-of-Pearl
Caterpillar

World's Longest
Insect Migration

Monarch Butterfly

The World's
LONGEST INSECT MIGRATIONS

Migrations in miles/kilometers

2,700 mi. 4,345 km.	2,600 mi. 4,184 km.	2,500 mi. 4,023 km.	1,850 mi. 2,977 km.	300 mi. 483 km.
Monarch Butterfly	Desert Locust	Painted Lady Butterfly	Diamondback Moth	Ladybug

Millions of monarch butterflies travel to Mexico from all parts of North America every fall, flying up to 2,700 miles (4,345 km). Once there, they will huddle together in the trees and wait out the cold weather. In spring and summer, most butterflies only live four or five weeks as adults, but in the fall, a special generation of monarchs is born. These butterflies will live for about seven months and participate in the great migration to Mexico. Scientists are studying these butterflies in hope of learning how the insects know where and when to migrate to a place they—or several generations before them—have never visited.

123

World's Tallest Mountain

Mount Everest

Mount Everest's tallest peak towers 29,035 feet (8,850 m) into the air, and it is the highest point on Earth. This peak is an unbelievable 5.5 miles (8.8 km) above sea level. Mount Everest is located in the Himalayas, on the border between Nepal and Tibet. The mountain got its official name from surveyor Sir George Everest. In 1953, Sir Edmund Hillary and Tenzing Norgay were the first people to reach the peak. In 2008, the Olympic torch will be carried up to the top of the mountain on its way to the games in Beijing.

The World's
TALLEST MOUNTAINS

Highest point in feet/meters

29,035 ft. 8,850 m.	28,250 ft. 8,611 m.	28,208 ft. 8,598 m.	27,923 ft. 8,516 m.	27,824 ft. 8,486 m.
Mount Everest, Asia	K2, Asia	Kangchenjunga, Asia	Lhotse, Asia	Makalu, Asia

World's Tallest Volcano

Ojos del Salado

The World's
TALLEST VOLCANOES

Height in feet/meters

22,595 ft. 6,887 m.	22,057 ft. 6,723 m.	21,850 ft. 6,660 m.	21,430 ft. 6,532 m.	20,922 ft. 6,398 m.
Ojos del Salado, Argentina/ Chile	Llullaillaco, Argentina/ Chile	Tipas, Argentina	Cerro El Condor, Argentina	Coropuna, Peru

Located on the border of Argentina and Chile, Ojos del Salado towers 22,595 feet (6,887 m) above the surrounding Atacama Desert. It is the second-highest peak in the Andean mountain chain. Ojos del Salado is a composite volcano, which means that it is a tall, symmetrical cone that was built by layers of lava flow, ash, and cinder. There is no record of the volcano erupting, but this could be because of the volcano's remote location. Ojos del Salado is a very popular spot for mountain climbing.

125

World's
Largest Lake

Caspian Sea

This giant inland body of saltwater stretches for almost 750 miles (1,207 km) from north to south, with an average width of about 200 miles (322 km). All together, it covers an area that's almost the same size as the state of California. The Caspian Sea is located east of the Caucasus Mountains in Central Asia. It is bordered by Iran, Russia, Kazakhstan, Azerbaijan, and Turkmenistan. The Caspian Sea has an average depth of about 550 feet (170 m). It is an important fishing resource, with species including sturgeon, salmon, perch, herring, and carp. Other animals live in the Caspian Sea, including porpoises, seals, and tortoises. The sea is estimated to be 30 million years old and became landlocked 5.5 million years ago.

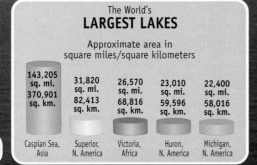

The World's
LARGEST LAKES

Approximate area in
square miles/square kilometers

143,205 sq. mi. 370,901 sq. km.	31,820 sq. mi. 82,413 sq. km.	26,570 sq. mi. 68,816 sq. km.	23,010 sq. mi. 59,596 sq. km.	22,400 sq. mi. 58,016 sq. km.
Caspian Sea, Asia	Superior, N. America	Victoria, Africa	Huron, N. America	Michigan, N. America

World's
Largest Desert

The Sahara

The World's
LARGEST DESERTS

Area in millions of
square miles/square kilometers

3.5 M sq. mi. 9.1 M sq. km.	1.4 M sq. mi. 3.6 M sq. km.	0.5 M sq. mi. 1.3 M sq. km.	0.4 M sq. mi. 1.0 M sq. km.	0.2 M sq. mi. 0.5 M sq. km.
Sahara, Africa	Australian, Australia	Arabian, Africa	Gobi, Asia	Kalahari, Africa

Located in northern Africa, the Sahara Desert covers approximately 3.5 million square miles (9.1 million sq km). It stretches for 5,200 miles (8,372 km) through the countries of Morocco, Algeria, Tunisia, Libya, Egypt, Mauritania, Mali, Niger, Chad, and Sudan. The Sahara gets very little rainfall—less than 8 inches (20 cm) per year. Even with its harsh environment, some 2.5 million people—mostly nomads—call the Sahara home. Date palms and acacias grow near oases. Some of the animals that live in the Sahara include gazelles, antelopes, jackals, foxes, and badgers.

World's
Longest River

The Nile River in Africa stretches 4,145 miles (6,671 km), from the tributaries of Lake Victoria in Tanzania and Uganda out to the Mediterranean Sea. Because of varying depths, boats can sail on only about 2,000 miles (3,217 km) of the river. The Nile flows through Rwanda, Uganda, Sudan, and Egypt. The river's water supply is crucial to the existence of these African countries. The Nile's precious water is used to irrigate crops and to generate electricity. The Aswan Dam and the Aswan High Dam—both located in Egypt—are used to store the autumn floodwater for later use. The Nile is also used to transport goods from city to city along the river.

The Nile

The World's
LONGEST RIVERS
Total length in miles/kilometers

4,145 mi. 6,671 km.	4,000 mi. 6,437 km.	3,740 mi. 6,021 km.	3,720 mi. 5,987 km.	3,650 mi. 5,877 km.
Nile, Africa	Amazon, S. America	Mississippi-Missouri, N. America	Yangtze, Asia	Yenisei, Angara, Asia

World's
Greatest-Flowing River

Amazon

The World's
GREATEST-FLOWING RIVERS
Average flow per second
in billions of gallons/cubic meters

Amazon, South America	Zaire, Africa	Negro, South America	Yangtze-Kiang, Asia	Orinoco, South America
58 B gal. 220,000 cu. m.	10.3 B gal. 39,000 cu. m.	9.2 B gal. 35,000 cu. m.	8.5 B gal. 32,190 cu. m.	6.7 B gal. 25,200 cu. m.

The Amazon River moves more water than any other river in the world. It empties 58 billion gallons (220,000 cu m) per second into the Atlantic Ocean. At 4,080 miles (6,566 km), the Amazon is the second-longest river in the world. It contains more water than the Nile, Mississippi, and Yangtze rivers combined, and makes up more than 20% of the Earth's fresh water. The Amazon is also the world's widest river, measuring up to 7 miles (11 km) from bank to bank. The mouth of the Amazon measures about 200 miles (322 km), and contains the Marajo—the world's largest freshwater island.

World's
Largest Ocean

Pacific

The Pacific Ocean covers almost 64 million square miles (166 million sq km) and reaches 36,200 feet (11,000 m) below sea level at its greatest depth—the Mariana Trench (near the Philippines). In fact, this ocean is so large that it covers about one-third of the planet (more than all of Earth's land put together) and holds more than half of all the seawater on Earth. The United States could fit inside this ocean 18 times! Some of the major bodies of water included in the Pacific are the Bering Sea, the Coral Sea, the Philippine Sea, and the Gulf of Alaska.

The World's
LARGEST OCEANS

Maximum area in millions of
square miles/square kilometers

64.0 M sq. mi.
165.7 M sq. km.

31.8 M sq. mi.
82.4 M sq. km.

25.3 M sq. mi.
65.5 M sq. km.

5.4 M sq. mi.
14.0 M sq. km.

Pacific Ocean   Atlantic Ocean   Indian Ocean   Arctic Ocean

World's Longest
Mountain Chain

The Andes

For 5,000 miles (8,050 km) the Andes extend through seven countries of South America—Venezuela, Colombia, Ecuador, Peru, Bolivia, Chile, and Argentina. The Andes also have some of the highest peaks in the world, with more than fifty of them measuring above 20,000 feet (6,100 m). Some of the animals found in the Andes include wild horses, vicuñas—members of the camel family, and chinchillas, furry members of the rodent family. The condor—the world's largest bird of prey—also calls these mountains its home.

The World's
LONGEST MOUNTAIN CHAINS

Length in miles/kilometers

Mountain Chain	Length
Andes, South America	5,000 mi. 8,050 km.
Transantarctic Mountains, Antarctica	2,200 mi. 3,542 km.
Rocky Mountains, USA	2,000 mi. 3,220 km.
Great Dividing Range, Australia	1,900 mi. 3,059 km.
Himalayas, Asia	1,600 mi. 2,576 km.

World's
Largest Island

Greenland

Located in the North Atlantic Ocean, Greenland covers more than 840,000 square miles (2,175,600 sq km). Not including continents, it is the largest island in the world. Its jagged coastline is approximately 24,400 miles (39,267 km) long—about the same distance as Earth's circumference at the equator. Mountain chains are located on Greenland's east and west coasts, and the coastline is indented by fjords, or thin bodies of water bordered by steep cliffs. From north to south, the island stretches for about 1,660 miles (2,670 km). About 700,000 square miles (1,813,000 sq km) of this massive island are covered by a giant ice sheet. The island also contains the world's largest national park—Northeast Greenland National Park—with an area of 375,291 square miles (972,000 sq km).

The World's
LARGEST ISLANDS

Approximate area in
square miles/square kilometers

Greenland	New Guinea	Borneo	Madagascar	Baffin Island
840,070 sq. mi. 2,175,600 sq. km.	312,190 sq. mi. 808,572 sq. km.	289,961 sq. mi. 751,000 sq. km.	226,674 sq. mi. 587,086 sq. km.	195,926 sq. mi. 507,448 sq. km.

Country with the Most
Tropical Rain Forests

Brazil

The Countries with the
MOST TROPICAL RAIN FORESTS

Area in square miles/square kilometers

Brazil, South America	Democratic Republic of Congo, Africa	Indonesia, Asia	Peru, South America	Bolivia, South America
1,158,165 sq. mi. 2,999,634 sq. km.	515,871 sq. mi. 1,336,099 sq. km.	341,681 sq. mi. 884,950 sq. km.	265,414 sq. mi. 687,419 sq. km.	226,796 sq. mi. 587,398 sq. km.

Brazil—a large, tropical country in South America—has more than 1.15 million square miles (2.99 million sq km) of rain forest. The tropical forests of the Amazon River are located in the northern and north-central areas of the country. Amazonia, the world's largest rain forest, spreads across half of Brazil. The rain forest is home to 2.5 million insects, 500 mammals, 300 other reptile species, and a third of the world's birds. The rain forest is threatened, however, by timber companies, the growing human population, and ranchers clearing land for their herds to graze.

Country with the Longest Coastline

Canada

The Countries with the LONGEST COASTLINES

Total coastline in miles/kilometers

Canada	Indonesia	Russia	Philippines	Japan
125,566 mi. 202,079 km.	33,999 mi. 54,717 km.	23,396 mi. 37,652 km.	22,559 mi. 36,305 km.	18,486 mi. 29,750 km.

Canada's coastline measures 125,566 miles (202,079 km) long. If someone walked 12.5 miles (20.1 km) a day, it would take him or her about 33 years to walk its length. This measurement includes the mainland coast, as well as the coasts of the offshore islands. Of all the provinces and territories, Nunavut has the most coastline with 70,777 miles (113,904 km). The Canadian coast is made up of sandy beaches, towering cliffs, mudflats, marshes, and rocky piles. It also touches three oceans: the Pacific, the Atlantic, and the Arctic.

World's Largest Diamond

Golden Jubilee

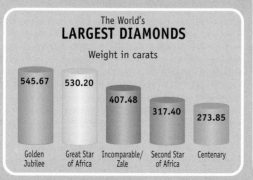

The World's
LARGEST DIAMONDS
Weight in carats

Golden Jubilee	Great Star of Africa	Incomparable/Zale	Second Star of Africa	Centenary
545.67	530.20	407.48	317.40	273.85

The Golden Jubilee is the world's largest faceted diamond with a weight of 545.67 carats. This gigantic gem got its name when it was presented to the king of Thailand in 1997 for the Golden Jubilee—or 50th anniversary celebration—of his reign. The diamond was discovered in a South African mine in 1986 weighing 755.5 carats. Once it was cut, the diamond featured 148 perfectly symmetrical facets. The process took almost a year because of the diamond's size and multiple tension points. The diamond is on display at the Royal Museum of Bangkok in Thailand.

135

World's Largest Fruit Crop

Tomatoes

More than 137 million tons (124 million t) of tomatoes are produced throughout the world each year. The world's top producers include the United States, Spain, Italy, Turkey, and China. Within the United States, about 130,700 acres (52,892 ha) are dedicated to growing the juicy, red fruit. California alone produces almost 1.5 billion pounds (680 M kg). There is occasionally some confusion about whether the tomato is a fruit or vegetable. This is usually because cooks use the tomato as a vegetable, but scientists classify it as a fruit.

The World's
LARGEST FRUIT CROPS

Production in
millions of tons/metric tons

Tomatoes	Watermelons	Bananas	Grapes	Apples
137.5 M tn 124.7 M t	105.1 M tn 95.3 M t	79.9 M tn 72.5 M t	73.7 M tn 66.9 M t	70.0 M tn 63.5 M t

World's
Largest Vegetable Crop

Sugar Cane

The World's
LARGEST VEGETABLE CROPS

Production in billions of tons/metric tons

1,425.5 B tons 1,293.2 B t.	Sugar Cane
354.8 B tons 321.9 B t.	Potatoes
266.6 B tons 241.9 B t.	Sugar Beets
143.2 B tons 129.9 B t.	Sweet Potatoes
120.7 B tons 109.5 B t.	Soybeans

More than 1.43 billion tons (1.29 B t) of sugar cane is produced worldwide each year. Sugar cane is a type of tropical grass which resembles bamboo. The stalk takes about a year to mature, and can grow to 16.5 feet (5 m) high. The stalks are shredded and crushed to extract the juice, which is then heated and cooled to form sugar crystals. Sugar cane is used to produce about 70% of the world's sugar. About 105 countries grow the crop, and the top producers are Brazil and India.

137

Country That Eats the
Most Vegetables

Greece

The people of Greece eat almost 622 pounds (282 kg) of vegetables each year. Some of the most popular vegetables in Greek cuisine include eggplants, okra, zucchini, potatoes, and green beans. Approximately four-fifths of Greece is mountainous, which makes farming difficult. Only about 3% of the cultivated areas can be used for vegetable crops. Most of the country's vegetables are grown in the plains of Thessaly, Macedonia, and Thrace.

The Countries That Eat the
MOST VEGETABLES

Annual consumption in pounds/kilograms

Greece	United Arab Emirates	China	Libya	Lebanon
622 lb. 282 kg.	575 lb. 261 kg.	564 lb. 256 kg.	534 lb. 242 kg.	523 lb. 237 kg.

Country That Eats the
Most Potato Chips

United Kingdom

People in the United Kingdom eat a lot of chips—averaging about 6.1 pounds (2.8 kg) per capita each year. That's enough chips to fill up more than 625 Olympic-sized swimming pools! Better known as "crisps" in the United Kingdom, potato chips were first served in 1853 at a lodge in Saratoga Springs, New York. It takes about 10,000 pounds (4,536 kg) of potatoes to make 3,500 pounds (1,588 kg) of chips.

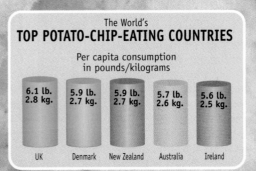

The World's
TOP POTATO-CHIP-EATING COUNTRIES

Per capita consumption
in pounds/kilograms

6.1 lb. 2.8 kg.	5.9 lb. 2.7 kg.	5.9 lb. 2.7 kg.	5.7 lb. 2.6 kg.	5.6 lb. 2.5 kg.
UK	Denmark	New Zealand	Australia	Ireland

139

Country That Drinks the
Most Bottled Water

Italy

Italians like their bottled water—each person in the country drinks almost 47 gallons (177 l) of it each year. That averages to about a bottle and a half each day. The total amount of bottled water consumed in Italy each year averages 2.6 billion gallons (9.8 B l). There are

The Countries That
DRINK THE MOST BOTTLED WATER
Annual consumption in gallons/liters

Italy	Spain	France	Mexico	Belgium
46.7 gal. 176.8 l.	41.4 gal. 156.7 l.	40.2 gal. 152.2 l.	40.1 gal. 151.8 l.	34.4 gal. 130.1 l.

Country That Consumes the
Most Soft Drinks

United States

Americans have an annual per capita soft drink consumption of 51.7 gallons (195.8 l). This means that each person in the country drinks an average of 551 cans of soda each year. Soda accounts for about 25% of all drinks consumed in the United States, and some 15.4 billion gallons (58.3 billion l) are sold annually. Recent studies show that diet sodas, as well as flavored sodas such as cherry, orange, and root beer, are becoming more popular than colas. The country's three top-selling soft drink companies are the Coca-Cola Company, PepsiCo Inc., and Dr Pepper/7UP.

The World's
TOP SODA-DRINKING COUNTRIES

Per capita consumption
in gallons/liters

USA	Mexico	Norway	Ireland	Canada
51.7 gal. 195.8 l.	33.3 gal. 126.0 l.	32.2 gal. 122.0 l.	32.1 gal. 121.4 l.	30.9 gal. 117.1 l.

141

Country That Eats the
Most Chocolate

Switzerland

The World's
TOP CHOCOLATE-EATING COUNTRIES

Annual chocolate consumption
per capita in pounds/kilograms

22.4 lb. 10.2 kg.	22.0 lb. 10.0 kg.	20.9 lb. 9.5 kg.	20.1 lb. 9.1 kg.	19.5 lb. 8.8 kg.
Switzerland	UK	Germany	Austria	Ireland

The per-capita chocolate consumption in Switzerland is 22.4 pounds (10.2 kg) per year. That means approximately 169 million pounds (76.7 million kg) of chocolate are eaten in this small country each year. In 2006, Switzerland produced more than 160,000 tons (145,150 t) of chocolate, and exported about 57% of it. Chocolate has always been a popular food around the world. In fact, each year, approximately 595,000 tons (539,775 t) of cocoa beans—an important ingredient in chocolate—are consumed worldwide. Chocolate is consumed mainly in the form of candy.

Country That Eats the Most Ice Cream

New Zealand

Each person in New Zealand eats an average of 55.6 pints (26.3 l) of ice cream every year. That's more than 1 pint per week. New Zealand also exports a lot of ice cream—about 26.7 million pounds (12.1 M kg) a year. The top flavors in New Zealand include vanilla, hokey pokey (vanilla with toffee bits), chocolate, and strawberry. Frozen treats were first served in the Roman Empire when people mixed fruit with ice. In the eighteenth century, ice cream became popular in France, England, and the United States. The ice-cream cone was first served in 1904 at the World's Fair in St. Louis, Missouri. Today, frozen dessert sales total billions of dollars worldwide.

The World's
TOP ICE-CREAM-EATING COUNTRIES

Per capita consumption in pints/liters

New Zealand	United States	Australia	Canada	Switzerland
55.6 pt. 26.3 l.	39.5 pt. 18.7 l.	37.6 pt. 17.8 l.	37.6 pt. 17.8 l.	29.8 pt. 14.1 l.

143

Country That Eats the Most Meat

Spain

Spain leads the pack in per capita meat consumption with 296 pounds (134 kg) per capita. That's like eating a quarter-pound burger with every meal for a year! The majority of meat—more than 70%—is eaten at lunchtime. Although the popularity of meat dishes in restaurants is on the rise, most meat is cooked and eaten at home. Meat consumption has been rising steadily over the last twenty years, as Spaniards moved away from the traditional vegetable-based Mediterranean diet.

The Countries with the HIGHEST MEAT CONSUMPTION

Annual consumption per capita in pounds/kilograms

Spain	Denmark	Australia	Ireland	USA
296 lb. 134 kg.	283 lb. 128 kg.	241 lb. 109 kg.	234 lb. 106 kg.	224 lb. 102 kg.

United States'
Greatest Snowfall

Mount Rainier

Mount Rainier had a record snowfall of 1,224 inches (3,109 cm) between 1971 and 1972. That's enough snow to cover a 10-story building! Located in the Cascade Mountains of Washington state, Mount Rainier is actually a volcano buried under 35 square miles (90.7 sq km) of snow and ice. The mountain, which covers about 100 square miles (259 sq km), reaches a height of 14,410 feet (4,392 m). Its three peaks include Liberty Cap, Point Success, and Columbia Crest. Mt. Rainier National Park was established in 1899.

United States'
GREATEST ANNUAL SNOWFALLS

Highest annual snowfall
in inches/centimeters

1,224 in. 3,109 cm.	1,140 in. 2,895 cm.	1,122 in. 2,849 cm.	974 in. 2,474 cm.
Mount Rainier, Washington, 1971–1972	Mount Baker, Washington, 1998–1999	Paradise Station, Washington, 1971–1972	Thompson Pass, Alaska, 1952–1953

World's Coldest Inhabited Place

Resolute

The residents of Resolute, Canada, have to bundle up—the average annual temperature is just -16° Fahrenheit (-26.6° C). Located on the northeast shore of Resolute Bay on the south coast of Cornwallis Island, the community is commonly the starting point for expeditions to the North Pole. In the winter it can stay dark for 24 hours, and in the summer it can stay light during the entire night. Fewer than 210 people brave the climate year-round, but the area is becoming quite popular with tourists.

The World's
COLDEST INHABITED PLACES

Average temperature in degrees
Fahrenheit/Celsius

Resolute, Canada	Eureka, Canada	Ostrov Bol'shoy, Russia	Point Barrow, Alaska, USA	Barter Island, Alaska, USA
-16° F -26.6° C	-3.5° F -19.7° C	5.5° F -14.7° C	9.8° F -12.3° C	10.2° F -12.1° C

World's Hottest
Inhabited Place

Dallol

The World's
HOTTEST INHABITED PLACES

Average temperature in degrees
Fahrenheit/Celsius

93.2° F 34.0° C	90.9° F 32.7° C	89.1° F 31.7° C	87.4° F 30.7° C	86.8° F 30.4° C
Dallol, Ethiopia	Bangkok, Thailand	Manila, Philippines	Singapore, Singapore	Assab, Eritrea

Throughout the year, temperatures in Dallol, Ethiopia, in Africa average 93.2° Fahrenheit (34.0° C). On some days it can reach 145° Fahrenheit (62.8° C) in the sun. Dallol is at the northernmost tip of the Great Rift Valley. The Dallol Depression reaches 328 feet (100 m) below sea level, making it the lowest point below sea level that is not covered by water. The area also has several active volcanoes. The only people to inhabit the region are the Afar, who have adapted to the harsh conditions there. For instance, to collect water the women build covered stone piles and wait for condensation to form on the rocks.

World's Wettest
Inhabited Place

Cherrapunji

Each year, some 498 inches (1,265 cm) of rain falls on Cherrapunji, India. That's enough rain to cover a four-story building! Most of the region's rain falls within a six-month period, during the monsoon season. It's not uncommon for constant rain to pelt the area for two months straight without even a 10-minute break. During the other six months, the winds change and carry the rain away from Cherrapunji, leaving the ground dry and dusty. Ironically, this causes a drought throughout most of the area.

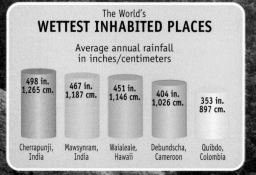

The World's
WETTEST INHABITED PLACES

Average annual rainfall
in inches/centimeters

498 in. 1,265 cm.	467 in. 1,187 cm.	451 in. 1,146 cm.	404 in. 1,026 cm.	353 in. 897 cm.
Cherrapunji, India	Mawsynram, India	Waialeale, Hawaii	Debundscha, Cameroon	Quibdo, Colombia

World's Driest Inhabited Place

Aswan

Each year, only .02 inches (.5 mm) of rain falls on Aswan, Egypt. In the country's sunniest and southernmost city, summer temperatures can reach a blistering 114° Fahrenheit (46° C). Aswan is located on the west bank of the Nile River. The Aswan High Dam, at 12,565 feet (3,830 m) long, is the city's most famous landmark. It produces the majority of Egypt's power in the form of hydroelectricity. Aswan also has many Pharaonic, Greco-Roman, and Muslim ruins.

The World's
DRIEST INHABITED PLACES

Average annual rainfall in inches/millimeters

Aswan, Egypt	Arica, Chile	Luxor, Egypt	Ica, Peru	Wadi Halfa, Sudan
0.02 in. 0.50 mm.	0.03 in. 0.76 mm.	0.03 in. 0.76 mm.	0.09 in. 2.3 mm.	0.10 in. 2.5 mm.

Place with the World's
Fastest Winds

Mount Washington

The World's
FASTEST WINDS

Speed of strongest winds
in miles/kilometers per hour

231 mph 372 kph	200 mph 322 kph	185 mph 298 kph	125 mph 201 kph	91 mph 146 kph
Mount Washington, New Hampshire, USA	Commonwealth Bay, Antarctica	South Pole, Antarctica	New Orleans, Louisiana, USA	Buffalo, New York, USA

The wind gusts at the top of Mount Washington reached 231 miles (372 km) per hour in 1934—and these gusts were not part of a storm. Normally, the average wind speed at the summit of this mountain is approximately 36 miles (58 km) per hour. Located in the White Mountains of New Hampshire, Mount Washington is the highest peak in New England at 6,288 feet (1,917 m). The treeless summit, which is known for its harsh weather, has an average annual temperature of only 26.5° Fahrenheit (-3.1° C).

World's Tallest Weed

Giant Hogweed

Growing to a height of 12 feet (3.6 m), the giant hogweed can have leaves that measure 3 feet (91 cm) long. This weed is taller than some trees! The giant hogweed is part of the parsley, or carrot, family and it has hollow stalks with tiny white flowers. Although it was first brought to America from Asia as an ornamental plant, the hogweed quickly became a pest. Each plant can produce about 50,000 seeds and the weed quickly spreads through its environment.

The World's TALLEST WEEDS

Average height in feet/meters

Giant Hogweed	Burdock	Giant Ragweed	Lambsquarters	Bull Thistle
12 ft. 3.6 m.	9 ft. 2.7 m.	8.9 ft. 2.7 m.	7 ft. 2.1 m.	6 ft. 1.8 m.

World's Largest Leaves

Raffia Palm

The raffia palm tree has leaves that reach lengths of 65 feet (19.8 m) long—about the same length as a regulation tennis court. Raffia trees have several stems that can reach heights of 6 to 30 feet (2 to 9 m). When they reach about 50 years of age, raffia palms flower and produce egg-size fruits covered in hard scales. Several products come from these palms, including raffia, and floor and shoe polish. Raffia leaves are also used to weave baskets, mats, and hats. These enormous plants are native to Madagascar, but most of the native growth has been overharvested. The palms are now cultivated in West and East Africa.

The World's
LARGEST LEAVES

Length in feet/meters

65 ft. 19.8 m.	20 ft. 6 m.	18 ft. 5.5 m.	16 ft. 5 m.	13 ft. 4 m.
Raffia Palm	Fan Palm	Date Palm	Coconut Palm	Oil Palm

World's Tallest Cactus

Saguaro

Many saguaro cacti grow to a height of 50 feet (15 m), but some have actually reached 75 feet (23 m). That's taller than a seven-story building. Saguaros start out quite small and grow very slowly. A saguaro only reaches about 1 inch (2.5 cm) high during its first 10 years. It will not bloom until it is between 50 and 75 years old. By this time, the cactus has a strong root system that can support about 9 to 10 tons (8 to 9 t) of growth. Its spines can measure up to 2.5 inches (5 cm) long. Saguaro cacti live for about 170 years. The giant cactus can be found from southeastern California to southern Arizona.

The World's
TALLEST CACTI

Height in feet/meters

Saguaro	Organ Pipe	Opuntia	Cane Cholla	Barrel
50–75 ft. 15–23 m.	40–50 ft. 12–15 m.	33 ft. 10 m.	30 ft. 9 m.	12 ft. 3.7 m.

Country That Produces the Most Fruit

China

Each year, China produces about 89 million tons (81 M t) of fruit—about 10% of the world's total fruit production. The country's fruit crop is worth about $15.2 billion annually. China is the world's top producer of apples and pears, and ranks third in the world for citrus fruit production. The country's orchards total about 22 million acres (8.9 M ha)—almost a quarter of the world's orchard land. More than half of China's population works in the agriculture industry.

The Countries that Produce the
MOST FRUIT

Millions of tons/metric tons produced annually

China	India	Brazil	USA	Italy
88.9 M tons 80.6 M t.	51.8 M tons 47.0 M t.	39.7 M tons 36.0 M t.	32.9 M tons 24.8 M t.	19.5 M tons 17.7 M t.

World's Tallest Tree

California Redwood

Growing in both California and southern Oregon, California redwoods can reach a height of 385 feet (117.4 m). Their trunks can grow up to 25 feet (7.6 m) in diameter. The tallest redwood on record stands 385 feet (117.4 m) tall—more than 60 feet (18.3 m) taller than the Statue of Liberty. Amazingly, this giant tree grows from a seed the size of a tomato. Some redwoods are believed to be more than 2,000 years old. The trees' thick bark and foliage protect them from natural hazards such as insects and fires.

The World's TALLEST TREE SPECIES

Height in feet/meters

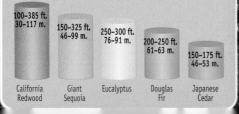

California Redwood	Giant Sequoia	Eucalyptus	Douglas Fir	Japanese Cedar
100–385 ft. 30–117 m.	150–325 ft. 46–99 m.	250–300 ft. 76–91 m.	200–250 ft. 61–63 m.	150–175 ft. 46–53 m.

World's Most
Poisonous Mushroom

Death Cap

The World's
MOST POISONOUS MUSHROOMS

Ranked 1–5 by likeliness to
cause death in humans

1	2	3	4	5
Death Cap	Destroying Angel	Amanita Alba	Fly Agaric	Deadly Galerina

Death cap mushrooms are members of the Amanita family, which are among the most dangerous mushrooms in the world. The death cap contains deadly peptide toxins that cause rapid loss of bodily fluids and intense thirst. Within six hours, the poison shuts down the kidneys, liver, and central nervous system, causing coma and—in more than 50% of cases—death. Estimates of the number of poisonous mushroom species range from 80 to 2,000. Most experts agree, however, that at least 100 varieties will cause severe symptoms and even death if eaten.

World's Largest Flower

Rafflesia

The World's LARGEST FLOWERS

Maximum flower size in inches/centimeters

Rafflesia	Sunflower	Giant Water Lily	Brazilian Dutchman	Magnolia
36 in. 91 cm.	19 in. 48 cm.	18 in. 46 cm.	14 in. 36 cm.	10 in. 25 cm.

The blossoms of the giant rafflesia—or "stinking corpse lily"—can reach 36 inches (91 cm) in diameter and weigh up to 25 pounds (11 kg). Its petals can grow 1.5 feet (0.5 m) long and 1 inch (2.5 cm) thick. There are 16 different species of Rafflesia. This endangered plant is found only in the rain forests of Borneo and Sumatra. It lives inside the bark of host vines and is noticeable only when its flowers break through to blossom. The large, reddish-purple flowers give off a smell similar to rotting meat, which attracts insects to help spread the rafflesia's pollen.

World's Deadliest Plant

Castor Bean Plant

The World's
DEADLIEST PLANTS
Risk of fatality if consumed

Extreme	High	High	Medium	Low
Castor Bean	Rosary Bead	Foxglove	Azalea	English Ivy

The castor bean plant produces seeds that contain a protein called ricin. Scientists estimate that ricin is about 6,000 times more poisonous than cyanide and 12,000 times more poisonous than rattlesnake venom. It would take a particle of ricin only about the size of a grain of sand to kill a 160-pound (73 kg) adult. The deadly beans are actually quite pretty and are sometimes used in jewelry. Castor bean plants grow in warmer climates and can reach a height of about 10 feet (3 m). Its leaves can measure up to 2 feet (0.6 m) wide.

World's Largest Seed

Coco de Mer

Some of the World's
LARGEST SEEDS
Length in inches/centimeters

12 in. 30 cm.	6 in. 15 cm.	3 in. 7.6 cm.	2 in. 3 cm.	1 in. 2.5 cm.
Coco de Mer	Coconut	Avocado	Peach	Acorn

Measuring 3 feet (1 m) in diameter and 12 inches (30 cm) in length, the giant, dark-brown seed of the coco de mer palm tree can weigh up to 40 pounds (18 kg). Only a few thousand seeds are produced each year. Coco de mer trees are found on the island of Praslin in the Seychelles Archipelago of the Indian Ocean. The area where some of the few remaining trees grow has been declared a Natural World Heritage Site in an effort to protect the species from poachers looking for the rare seeds. The tree can grow up to 100 feet (31 m) tall, with leaves measuring 20 feet (6 m) long and 12 feet (3.6 m) wide.

World's Highest Tsunami Wave Since 1900

Lituya Bay

A 1,720-foot- (524-m-) high tsunami wave crashed down in Lituya Bay, Alaska, on July 9, 1958. Located in Glacier Bay National Park, the tsunami was caused by a massive landslide that was triggered by an 8.3 magnitude earthquake. The water from the bay covered 5 square miles (13 sq km) of land and traveled inland as far as 3,600 feet (1,097 m). Millions of trees were washed away. Amazingly, because the area was very isolated and the coastline was sheltered by coves, only two people died when their fishing boat sank.

The World's
HIGHEST TSUNAMI WAVES SINCE 1900

Height of wave in feet/meters

1,720 ft. 524 m.				
	75 ft. 23 m.	60 ft. 18 m.	50 ft. 15 m.	20 ft. 6 m.
Lituya Bay, Alaska, USA, 1958	Chile, 1960	The Philipphines, 1960	Southern Asia, 2004	Alaska, USA, 1964

World's Most Intense
Earthquake Since 1900

Coastal Chile

The World's
MOST INTENSE EARTHQUAKES SINCE 1900

Magnitude

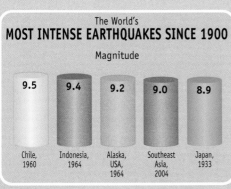

9.5	9.4	9.2	9.0	8.9
Chile, 1960	Indonesia, 1964	Alaska, USA, 1964	Southeast Asia, 2004	Japan, 1933

An explosive earthquake measuring 9.5 on the Richter scale rocked the coast of Chile on May 22, 1960. This is equal to the intensity of about 60,000 hydrogen bombs. Some 2,000 people were killed and another 3,000 injured. The death toll was fairly low because the foreshocks frightened people into the streets. When the massive jolt came, many of the collapsed buildings were already empty. The coastal towns of Valdivia and Puerto Montt suffered the most damage because they were closest to the epicenter—located about 100 miles (161 km) offshore.

World's Most Destructive
Flood Since 1900

Hurricane Katrina

The pounding rain and storm surges of Hurricane Katrina resulted in catastrophic flooding that cost about $60 billion. The storm formed in late August 2005 over the Bahamas, moved across Florida, and finally hit Louisiana on August 29 as a category 3 storm. The storm surge from the Gulf of Mexico flooded the state, as well as neighboring Alabama and Mississippi. Many levees could not hold back the massive amounts of water, and entire towns were destroyed. In total, some 1,800 people lost their lives.

The World's
MOST DESTRUCTIVE FLOODS SINCE 1900

Cost of damages, in billions of US dollars

$60.0B	$30.0B	$27.0B	$24.0B	$18.0B
Hurricane Katrina, USA, 2005	Yangtze River, China, 1998	Bangladesh, 1970	Yangtze River, China, 1990	Great Midwest Flood, USA, 1993

World's
Worst Oil Spill

On March 16, 1978, the *Amoco Cadiz* hit ground in shallow water off the coast of Brittany, France and spilled 220,000 tons (199,581 t) of oil into the English Channel. The very large crude carrier encountered strong storms and lost the ability to steer. Tug boats and the ship's anchor were unable to stop the tanker from drifting, and it collided with the rocky shore. The ship's hull and storage tanks were ripped open, and 68.7 million gallons (260 million l) of oil spread across 125 miles (201 km) of the Brittany coastline. The oil slick ruined fisheries, oyster beds, and surrounding beaches.

The World's
WORST OIL SPILLS

Oil spilled, in tons/metric tons

Amoco Cadiz, Brittany, France 1978	Atlantic Empress, Tobago, 1979	Torrey Canyon, Isles of Scilly, UK, 1967	Braer, Shetland Isles UK, 1993	Sea Empress, Milford Haven, UK, 1996
220,000 tons 199,581 t.	160,000 tons 145,150 t.	119,000 tons 107,955 t.	85,000 tons 77,111 t.	72,000 tons 65,317 t.

Amoco Cadiz

163

World's Most Destructive
Tornado Since 1900

Oklahoma City

On May 3, 1999, a devastating tornado swept through downtown Oklahoma City, Oklahoma, killing 36 people and causing more than $1.2 billion in damages. This powerful twister traveled almost 38 miles (61 km) in four hours and measured a mile (1.6 km) wide at times. With raging winds reaching 318 miles (512 km) per hour, it was the strongest wind speed ever recorded. More than 800 houses were destroyed in Oklahoma City alone. Because of the mass destruction caused by this twister, it was classified as a five—the second-highest possible rating—on the Fujita Tornado Scale.

The World's
MOST DESTRUCTIVE TORNADOES SINCE 1900

Cost of damages in millions
and billions of US dollars

$1.2B	$1.1B	$1.0B	$650M	$450M
Oklahoma City, OK, 1999	Omaha, NE, 1975	Missouri, Illinois, Indiana, 1925	Southern United States, 2006	Pennsylvania, Ohio, 1985

World's Most Intense
Hurricane Since 1900

Hurricane Gilbert

The World's
MOST INTENSE HURRICANES SINCE 1900

Highest sustained wind speed
in miles/kilometers per hour

184 mph 296 kph	180 mph 290 kph	175 mph 282 kph	165 mph 266 kph	165 mph 266 kph
Hurricane Gilbert, 1988	Hurricane Mitch, 1998	Hurricane Katrina, 2005	Hurricane Allen, 1980	Hurricane Camille, 1969

During mid-September 1988, Hurricane Gilbert blew through the Atlantic, Caribbean, and Gulf of Mexico, destroying almost everything in its path. It devastated most of the island of Jamaica on September 10th, and later caused major flooding in the Yucatán Peninsula and in Northern Mexico five days later. Gilbert was classified as a category five hurricane—the most destructive hurricane rating on the Saffir-Simpson Hurricane Scale—for five days. The storm's top wind speeds reached 184 miles (296 km) per hour. The total clean-up cost for the hurricane was more than $5 billion. Some 318 people also lost their lives in the terrible storm.

Popular Culture Records

Television • Music • Theater
Movies • Books • Art

Most Popular
Television Show

American Idol—Tuesday

Tuesday's *American Idol* competition had the largest television audience in 2006, with 17.6% of TV viewers tuning in to watch. The show begins the season by holding auditions throughout the United States, looking for the next big singing sensation. After the semifinalists are picked by judges Simon Cowell, Randy Jackson, and Paula Abdul, television viewers narrow the competition down to 12 finalists by calling in to cast votes for their favorite singers. The contestant with the lowest votes is eliminated until one is left. The 2006 *American Idol* was Taylor Hicks, and Katharine McPhee was the runner-up.

Most Popular
TELEVISION SHOWS

Average audience percentage in 2006

American Idol Tuesday	American Idol Wednesday	CSI	Desperate Housewives	Grey's Anatomy
17.6%	17.2%	15.6%	13.8%	12.5%

Highest-Paid TV Actor

Kiefer Sutherland

Kiefer Sutherland became the best-paid actor on television when he signed a three-year deal worth $40 million to star in *24*. That averages out to $555,555 per episode! Sutherland plays federal agent Jack Bauer, a crime-fighting hero who battles domestic terrorism. *24* is unique in that every episode in the season portrays one hour of one day. Since the show began in 2001, Sutherland has won a Golden Globe, an Emmy Award, and a Screen Actor's Guild Award for his performance.

Highest-Paid
TV ACTORS

Money earned per episode during
the 2006–2007 season, in US dollars

Kiefer Sutherland, 24	Donald Trump, The Apprentice	Charlie Sheen, Two and a Half Men	Gary Sinise, CSI: New York	Matthew Fox, Lost
$555,555	$375,000	$350,000	$175,000	$90,400

Highest-Paid
TV Actresses

The Desperate Housewives

Highest-Paid
TV ACTRESSES

Money earned per episode during the
2006–2007 season, in US dollars

$440,000	$440,000	$440,000	$440,000	
				$300,000
Marcia Cross, *Desperate Housewives*	Teri Hatcher, *Desperate Housewives*	Felicity Huffman, *Desperate Housewives*	Eva Longoria, *Desperate Housewives*	Kyra Sedgwick, *The Closer*

Marcia Cross, Teri Hatcher, Felicity Huffman, and Eva Longoria—the main cast of the hit show *Desperate Housewives*—each make $440,000 an episode. The ladies of Wisteria Lane are better known as Bree Van De Kamp (Cross), Susan Mayer (Hatcher), Lynette Scavo (Huffman), and Gabrielle Solis (Longoria) to television audiences. Executive producer Marc Cherry brought this nighttime soap to life in 2004, and since then the show has won six Emmy Awards and two Golden Globes.

Highest-Paid Talk Show Host

Oprah Winfrey

Oprah Winfrey pulled in $225 million in 2006, making her the world's top-paid entertainer. In total, she is worth more than $1.2 billion. Oprah's self-made millions have come mostly from her television show, which began in 1983. Since then, Oprah has been educating her viewers and helping her audience with tough social issues. The megastar is also involved in movies, television production, magazines, books, radio, and the Internet. Oprah is also known for her great generosity, and has donated millions to various charities.

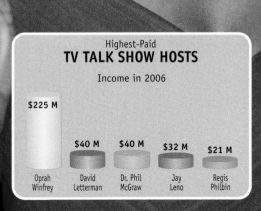

Highest-Paid
TV TALK SHOW HOSTS
Income in 2006

Oprah Winfrey	David Letterman	Dr. Phil McGraw	Jay Leno	Regis Philbin
$225 M	$40 M	$40 M	$32 M	$21 M

United States' Best-Selling
Male Recording Artist

Elvis Presley

Elvis Presley has sold more than 116.5 million records since he first signed with RCA Records back in 1955. Presley's unique sound and dance moves captured fans' attention around the world. Known as the King of Rock and Roll, Presley also holds the record for the solo singer with the most chart hits at 151. Some of his most famous songs include "Love Me Tender," "Blue Suede Shoes," "Jailhouse Rock," and "All Shook Up." Presley also had an impressive film career. He appeared in more than 30 films, which earned a combined total of about $150 million at the box office. Presley died in 1977.

The United States' Best-Selling
MALE RECORDING ARTISTS

Albums sold, in millions

Elvis Presley	Garth Brooks	Billy Joel	Elton John	George Strait
118.5 M	116.0 M	79.5 M	69.0 M	62.5 M

United States' Best-Selling
Female Recording Artist

Barbra Streisand

Barbra Streisand has sold almost 71 million copies of her work during her 39 years as a singer. She has recorded more than 50 albums and has more gold albums—or albums that have sold at least 500,000 copies—than any other entertainer in history. Streisand has 47 gold albums, 28 platinum albums, and 13 multiplatinum albums. Some of her recordings include "I Finally Found Someone" (1996), "Tell Him" (1997), and "If You Ever Leave Me" (1999). Some of her best-known film work includes roles in *Funny Girl, The Way We Were, Yentl,* and *Meet the Fockers.* Streisand has won 10 Grammys®, 2 Academy Awards®, 6 Emmy® Awards, and 11 Golden Globes.

The United States' Best-Selling
FEMALE RECORDING ARTISTS
Albums sold, in millions

Barbra Streisand	Madonna	Mariah Carey	Whitney Houston	Celine Dion
71.0 M	63.0 M	61.5 M	54.0 M	49.0 M

World's Top-Earning Male Singer

Bruce Springsteen

Bruce Springsteen took home $55 million in 2006. Springsteen's last two albums have been extremely successful. His *Devils & Dust* album went platinum with sales exceeding 625,000 copies. His follow-up, the critically acclaimed *We Shall Overcome: The Seeger Sessions*, showcases Springsteen's version of 13 classic songs by folk singer Pete Seeger. Springsteen's last tour also grossed more than $26 million.

The World's Top-Earning
MALE SINGERS OF 2006

Income in
millions of US dollars

$55 M

Bruce
Springsteen

$41 M

50 Cent

$40 M

Paul
McCartney

$35 M

Neil
Diamond

$34 M

Elton
John

World's Top-Earning Female Singer

Madonna

Madonna earned $108.3 million in 2006. Her "Confessions On a Dance Floor" tour grossed $97.1 million in 2006, with an average ticket price of $184—the second-highest price of any concert that year. The tour also increased album sales by half a million, contributing $11.2 million to her total income. Since the Material Girl began touring more than 20 years ago, she has grossed more than $1 billion. *Forbes Magazine* recently ranked her the richest female singer in the world, as well as the fourth-richest woman in entertainment.

The World's Top-Earning
FEMALE SINGERS OF 2006

Income in millions
of US dollars

$97.1 M	$92.5 M	$85.4 M	$54.2 M	$41.4 M
Madonna	Barbra Streisand	Celine Dion	Mariah Carey	Shania Twain

United States' Best-Selling Recording Group

The Beatles

The Beatles have sold 169 million copies of their music since their first official recording session in September 1962. In the two years that followed, they had 26 Top 40 singles. John Lennon, Paul McCartney, George Harrison, and Ringo Starr made up the "Fab Four," as the Beatles were known. Together they recorded many albums that are now considered rock masterpieces, such as *Rubber Soul, Sgt. Pepper's Lonely Hearts Club Band,* and *The Beatles.* The group broke up in 1969. In 2001, however, their newly released greatest hits album—*The Beatles 1*—reached the top of the charts. One of their best-known songs— "Yesterday"—is the most recorded song in history, with about 2,500 different artists recording their own versions.

The United States' BEST-SELLING RECORDING GROUP

Millions of albums sold

The Beatles	Led Zeppelin	The Eagles	Pink Floyd	AC/DC
169.0 M	109.5 M	91.0 M	73.5 M	68.0 M

Male Singer with the
Most Chart Hits

Elvis Presley

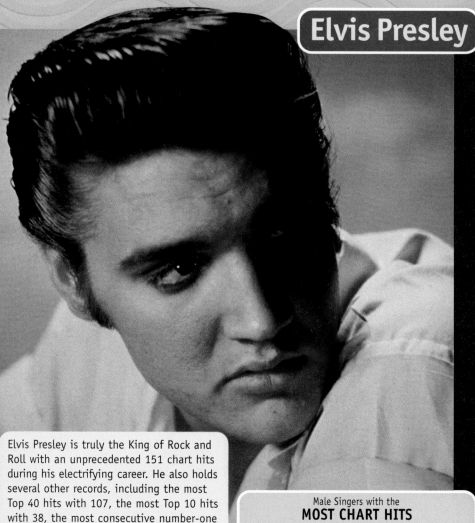

Elvis Presley is truly the King of Rock and Roll with an unprecedented 151 chart hits during his electrifying career. He also holds several other records, including the most Top 40 hits with 107, the most Top 10 hits with 38, the most consecutive number-one hits with 10, and the most weeks at number one with 80. Influenced by gospel, blues, and jazz, some of Presley's greatest hits include "Don't Be Cruel," "Hound Dog," "Heartbreak Hotel," and "Are You Lonesome Tonight?" And Elvis remains popular today—a greatest-hits album was released twenty-five years after his death and reached number one on the U.S. and U.K. charts.

Male Singers with the
MOST CHART HITS

Career chart hits

Elvis Presley	James Brown	Ray Charles	Elton John	Frank Sinatra
151	94	76	69	67

Female Singer with the Most Chart Hits

Aretha Franklin

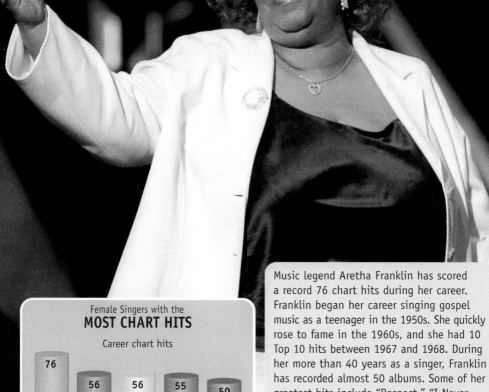

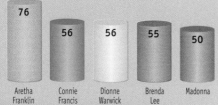

Female Singers with the MOST CHART HITS

Career chart hits

Aretha Franklin	Connie Francis	Dionne Warwick	Brenda Lee	Madonna
76	56	56	55	50

Music legend Aretha Franklin has scored a record 76 chart hits during her career. Franklin began her career singing gospel music as a teenager in the 1950s. She quickly rose to fame in the 1960s, and she had 10 Top 10 hits between 1967 and 1968. During her more than 40 years as a singer, Franklin has recorded almost 50 albums. Some of her greatest hits include "Respect," "I Never Loved a Man," "I Say a Little Prayer," and "Bridge Over Troubled Water." The Queen of Soul became the first woman inducted into the Rock and Roll Hall of Fame in 1987.

World's Top-Earning Band

The Rolling Stones

The Rolling Stones again claimed the record for the highest-grossing concert of 2006 with ticket sales totaling $138.5 million. Tickets to see the legendary rock group average $136 apiece and a total of 1.01 million were sold. The tour continued to promote the group's new album, *The Bigger Bang*—the Stones' first new album in eight years. Some of the new songs include "Streets of Love," "Rough Justice," and "Back of My Hand." In 2006, the Stones also rocked the crowd during halftime at Super Bowl XL.

The World's Top-Earning
BANDS OF 2006

Earnings in millions
of US dollars

Band	Earnings
The Rolling Stones	$138.5 M
Bon Jovi	$131.0 M
U2	$96.0 M
Dave Matthews Band	$58.0 M
Aerosmith	$58.0 M

Singer with the Most
Country Music Awards

Vince Gill

Since his debut album *Turn Me Loose* in 1984, country superstar Vince Gill has won 19 Country Music Awards. He won his first Country Music Award in 1990 for Single of the Year with "When I Call Your Name." Since then, he has won Male Vocalist of the Year five times, Song of the Year four times, Vocal Event of the Year four times, Entertainer of the Year twice, and Album of the Year twice. Gill also hosted the Country Music Awards from 1992 to 2003. Some of Gill's most successful albums include *The Key* (1998), and *Next Big Thing* (2003).

Singers with the Most
COUNTRY MUSIC AWARDS
Number of awards

19	17	16	11	10
Vince Gill	Brooks & Dunn	Alan Jackson	Garth Brooks	Dixie Chicks

Play with the
Most Tony Awards

The Producers

In March 2001, *The Producers* took home 12 of its record-breaking 15 Tony® nominations. The Broadway smash won awards for Best Musical, Best Original Score, Best Book, Best Direction of a Musical, Best Choreography, Best Orchestration, Best Scenic Design, Best Costume Design, Best Lighting Design, Best Actor in a Musical, Best Featured Actor in a Musical, and Best Actress in a Musical. *The Producers,* which starred Nathan Lane and Matthew Broderick, is a stage adaptation of Mel Brooks's 1968 movie. Brooks wrote the lyrics and music for 16 new songs for the stage version.

Plays with the
MOST TONY AWARDS

Number of Tony Awards

12	10	7	6	6
The Producers, 2001	Hello Dolly, 1964	The Phantom of the Opera, 1988	The History Boys, 2006	The Light in the Piazza, 2005

World's Longest-Running
Broadway Show

Phantom of the Opera

The Phantom of the Opera has been performed more than 7,901 times since the show opened in January 1988. The show tells the story of a disfigured musical genius who terrorizes the performers of the Paris Opera House. More than 80 million people have seen a performance, and box-office receipts total more than $3.2 billion. The show won seven Tony Awards its opening year, including Best Musical. The musical drama is performed at the Majestic Theatre.

The World's Longest-Running
BROADWAY SHOWS

Total performances*

7,901	7,485	6,680	6,137	5,959
The Phantom of the Opera, 1988–	Cats, 1982–2000	Les Misérables, 1987–2003	A Chorus Line, 1975–1990	Oh! Calcutta!, 1969–1972

*As of January 12, 2007

Actor with the Highest Career
Box-Office Earnings

Frank Welker

Frank Welker's movies have a combined total gross of $4.71 billion dollars. Although movie fans might not recognize Welker's name or face, they would probably recognize one of his voices. Welker is a voice actor, and has worked on 89 movies in the last 25 years. Some of his most famous voices include Megatron, Curious George, and Scooby-Doo. Some of Welker's most profitable movies include *How the Grinch Stole Christmas*, *Godzilla*, and *101 Dalmations*.

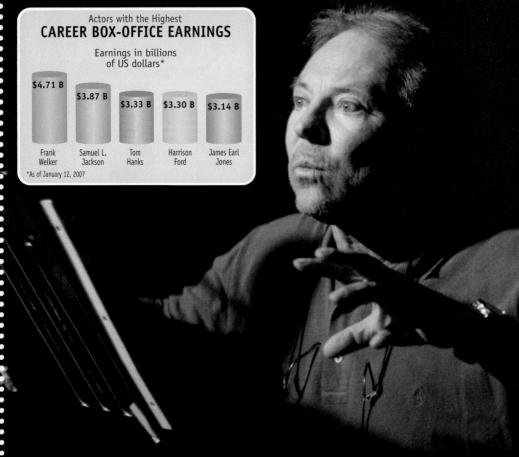

Actors with the Highest
CAREER BOX-OFFICE EARNINGS

Earnings in billions
of US dollars*

Frank Welker	Samuel L. Jackson	Tom Hanks	Harrison Ford	James Earl Jones
$4.71 B	$3.87 B	$3.33 B	$3.30 B	$3.14 B

*As of January 12, 2007

World's Top-Grossing
Kids' Movie

Snow White and the Seven Dwarfs

The World's
TOP-GROSSING KIDS' MOVIES

Box-office receipts in billions and
millions of dollars adjusted for inflation

$1.03 B	$977 M	$921 M	$892 M	$879 M
Snow White and the Seven Dwarfs, 1937	Harry Potter and the Sorcerer's Stone, 2001	Shrek 2, 2004	Harry Potter and the Goblet of Fire, 2005	Harry Potter and the Chamber of Secrets, 2002

Walt Disney's *Snow White and the Seven Dwarfs* has earned an amazing $1.03 billion in box-office receipts in the 69 years since its debut. (To compare the success of films throughout the decades, it is necessary to adjust for inflation.) More than 750 artists were used during the three-year production. *Snow White and the Seven Dwarfs* was the first-ever animated feature film, and it cost $1.4 million to make. Many of the songs in the movie, including "Some Day My Prince Will Come" and "Whistle While You Work," have become true American classics.

Most Successful Movie
Opening Weekend

Pirates of the Caribbean: Dead Man's Chest

Pirates of the Caribbean: Dead Man's Chest grossed $135.6 million during its opening weekend on July 7, 2006. A follow-up to 2003's highly successful *Pirates of the Caribbean: The Curse of The Black Pearl*, the sequel went on to gross $423.4 million in the United States and $1.06 billion worldwide. *Dead Man's Chest* stars Johnny Depp as Captain Jack Sparrow, Orlando Bloom as Will Turner, and Keira Knightley as Elizabeth Swann. The third and final movie in the trilogy—*Pirates of the Caribbean: At World's End*— was released in May 2007.

Movies with the
BEST OPENING WEEKENDS
Weekend earnings in millions of US dollars

$135.6 M	$114.8 M	$108.4 M	$108.0 M	$102.8 M
Pirates of the Caribbean: Dead Man's Chest 7/7/06	Spider-Man 5/3/02	Star Wars: Episode III— Revenge of the Sith 5/19/05	Shrek 2 5/19/04	X-Men: The Last Stand 5/26/06

Movies with the Most Oscars®

Ben-Hur, The Lord of the Rings: The Return of the King, Titanic

Movies with the MOST OSCAR® WINS

Oscars® won

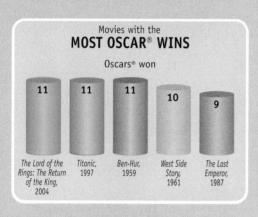

11	11	11	10	9
The Lord of the Rings: The Return of the King, 2004	Titanic, 1997	Ben-Hur, 1959	West Side Story, 1961	The Last Emperor, 1987

Cast and crew members with some of the 11 Oscars® for *The Lord of the Rings: The Return of the King*

The only three films in Hollywood history to win 11 Academy Awards® are *Ben-Hur, The Lord of the Rings: The Return of the King,* and *Titanic*. Some of the Oscar® wins for *Ben-Hur*—a biblical epic based on an 1880 novel by General Lew Wallace—include Best Actor (Charlton Heston) and Director. *The Lord of the Rings: The Return of the King* is the final film in the epic trilogy based on the works of J.R.R. Tolkien. With 11 awards, it is the most successful movie in Academy Awards® history because it won in every category in which it was nominated. Some of these wins include Best Picture, Best Director (Peter Jackson), and Best Costume Design. Some of *Titanic's* Oscars® include Cinematography, Visual Effects, and Costume Design.

Top
Moviegoing Country

Iceland

Iceland residents must love the silver screen—each person sees an average of 5.2 movies annually. There are just 22 cinemas and 46 cinema halls in the country with a combined seating capacity of 8,046. About three-quarters of the films shown in the country are produced in the United States, with just a handful of Icelandic films screened there. In fact, 9 out of the top 10 films that drew the highest attendance in Iceland were from the United States. Gross box office revenue averages $956,000 annually.

Top
MOVIEGOING COUNTRIES

Annual movies seen per capita

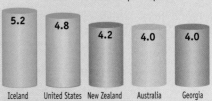

Iceland	United States	New Zealand	Australia	Georgia
5.2	4.8	4.2	4.0	4.0

Country with the
Most Movie Theaters

United States

There are more than 61,000 movie theaters with 37,100 screens throughout the country. Since the first permanent electric theater opened in 1902, Americans have flocked to the big screen. Megaplexes, or large movie theaters that show several movies at the same time, are the most popular type of theater in the country. Approximately 1.4 billion movie tickets are sold in the United States each year, with an average price of $6.41.

Countries with the
MOST MOVIE THEATERS

Number of movie screens

United States	India	Ukraine	Germany	Belarus
37,100	11,600	7,800	4,700	3,800

Highest
Animated Film Budget

The Polar Express

The Polar Express went into production with an unprecedented budget of $150 million. Its final production cost totaled $170 million. The film used new computer-generated technology called performance capture, giving the animation an incredibly realistic look. The animated film is based on the popular children's book about a magical train headed toward the North Pole on Christmas Eve. Several characters in the movie are voiced by Tom Hanks. The film has made more than $150 million since its release in 2004.

Highest
ANIMATED FILM BUDGETS

Budgets, in millions of US dollars

$170.0 M — The Polar Express, 2004
$145.0 M — Tarzan, 1999
$137.0 M — Final Fantasy: The Spirits Within, 2001
$127.5 M — Dinosaur, 2000
$115.0 M — Monsters, Inc., 2001

Highest-Paid
Director/Producer

Steven Spielberg

Steven Spielberg earned $332 million in 2006. One of the world's most well-known producers, Spielberg created *Letters From Iwo Jima, Flags of Our Fathers, Spell Your Name*, and *Monster House* in 2006. Spielberg began his directorial career in 1961. After working in television for several years, his first major film success was *Jaws* in 1975. Spielberg went on to create some of the most popular movies in history, including *Raiders of the Lost Ark* (1981), *E.T. The Extra-Terrestrial* (1982), *Schindler's List* (1993), *Men in Black* (1997), *Saving Private Ryan* (1998), and *Shrek* (2001).

Highest-Paid
DIRECTORS/PRODUCERS

Income in 2006

$332 M	$235 M	$84 M	$44 M	$39 M
Steven Spielberg	George Lucas	Jerry Bruckheimer	Mel Gibson	Peter Jackson

World's Highest-Paid Actor

Tom Cruise

Tom Cruise earned $79 million for reprising his role as Ethan Hunt in *Mission: Impossible III* in 2006. Cruise actually turned down an upfront salary for his work, opting for 20% of the movie's profits. Although the movie did not do nearly as well as expected at the box office, it still pulled in $395 million worldwide. Cruise also holds the record for the highest salary ever earned by an actor when he made approximately $100 million off *The War of the Worlds* profits. Forbes ranked Cruise the most powerful star of 2006.

The World's
HIGHEST-PAID ACTORS OF 2006

Salary in millions of US dollars

$79 M	$25 M	$20 M	$18 M	$17 M
Tom Cruise, *Mission: Impossible III*	Will Smith, *The Pursuit of Happyness*	Tom Hanks, *The Da Vinci Code*	Will Ferrell, *Talladega Nights: The Ballad of Ricky Bobby*	Johnny Depp, *Pirates of the Caribbean: Dead Man's Chest*

World's Highest-Paid Actress

Nicole Kidman

Nicole Kidman led the pack of Hollywood starlets in 2006, fetching $17 million per movie. Kidman earned the big bucks for her role as a psychiatrist in the sci-fi thriller *The Invasion*. Kidman also holds the record for the highest-paid actress in a commercial. She was paid a whopping $3.71 million to star in a 4-minute advertisement for Chanel perfume. Some of Kidman's other well-known movies include *Moulin Rouge!* (2001), *The Others* (2001), *The Hours* (2002), and *Cold Mountain* (2003).

The World's
HIGHEST-PAID ACTRESSES OF 2006

Approximate salary per movie, in millions of US dollars

$17.0 M	$15.0 M	$15.0 M	$15.0 M	$15.0 M
Nicole Kidman, *The Invasion*	Drew Barrymore, *Music and Lyrics*	Cameron Diaz, *Holiday*	Reese Witherspoon, *Penelope*	Renée Zellweger, *Miss Potter*

World's Top-Grossing
Movie

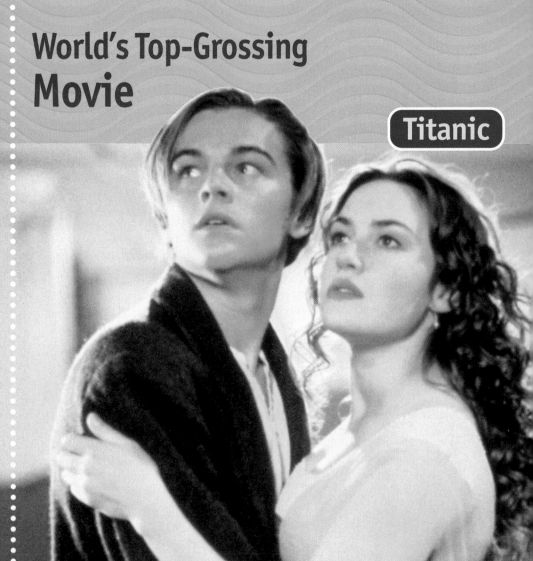

Titanic

Directed by James Cameron in 1997, *Titanic* has grossed more than $600 million in the United States and more than $1.8 billion worldwide. This action-packed drama/romance is set aboard the White Star Line's lavish *RMS Titanic* in 1912. The two main characters, wealthy Rose DeWitt Bukater and the poor immigrant Jack Dawson—played by Kate Winslet and Leonardo DiCaprio—meet, fall in love, and are separated as the *Titanic* sinks into the North Atlantic on the morning of April 15, 1912.

The World's
TOP-GROSSING MOVIES

Gross income, in billions and millions of US dollars

$1.85 B	$1.13 B	$1.06 B	$977 M	$926 M
Titanic, 1997	Lord of the Rings: The Return of the King, 2003	Pirates of the Caribbean: Dead Man's Chest, 2006	Harry Potter and the Sorcerer's Stone, 2001	Lord of the Rings: The Two Towers, 2002

World's Highest-Paid Author

Dan Brown

World-renowned author Dan Brown earned $88 million in 2006. Most of this income was from sales of his highly successful book *The Da Vinci Code*. *The Da Vinci Code* has spent more than 44 months on the *New York Times* bestseller list. It has sold more than 61 million copies worldwide and was made into a major motion picture in 2006. Three of the author's other bestsellers include *Angels & Demons, Digital Fortress,* and *Deception Point*. During one week in 2004, all four of Brown's novels were on the *New York Times* bestseller list.

The World's HIGHEST-PAID AUTHORS

Income 2006

Dan Brown	J.K. Rowling	Rick Warren	James Patterson	John Grisham
$88 M	$75 M	$28 M	$25 M	$21 M

World's
Most Sucessful Artist

Pablo Picasso

Pablo Picasso's work has earned more than $1.399 billion through sales and auctions. In fact, the most expensive painting ever sold was Picasso's "Boy with a Pipe" that brought in $104 million in 2004. The Spanish painter lived from 1881 to 1973. Most of Picasso's career is divided into periods according to the colors and styles he used. First came his Blue Period (1901 to 1904), followed by his Rose Period (1905 to 1907), then his African-influenced period (1908 to 1909), leading to his Analytic Cubism Period (1909 to 1912), and finally his Synthetic Cubism Period (1912 to 1919).

The World's
MOST SUCCESSFUL ARTISTS

Total value of work, in billions and millions of US dollars

Pablo Picasso	Claude Monet	Pierre-Auguste Renoir	Vincent van Gogh	Paul Cézanne
$1.399 B	$1.016 B	$664 M	$552 M	$486 M

Money Records

Industry • Wealth • Most Valuable

World's
Top-Selling Car

Toyota Camry

The World's
TOP-SELLING CARS
Total sold in 2006

Toyota Camry	Honda Accord	Honda Civic	Chevrolet Impala	Toyota Corolla
448,445	354,441	316,638	289,868	272,327

The Toyota Camry was the most popular car in 2006, with sales totaling almost 448,500 vehicles. The Camry has a standard 2.4-litre, 16-valve engine and features cruise control, keyless entry, and a state-of-the-art audio system. The Camry has also been rated as one of the safest cars on the road. In addition to front, overhead, and side-impact airbags, the car features Vehicle Skid Control brakes.

World's
Most Profitable Company

ExxonMobil

Gasoline giant ExxonMobil made a ton of cash in 2006, raking in more than $39.5 billion. The company recorded some $335 billion in sales. ExxonMobil produces, transports, and sells crude oil and natural gas worldwide. They also manufacture and sell petroleum products across the globe. In addition, Mobil 1 is the world's most successful motor oil. ExxonMobil has forty oil refineries in twenty countries and is capable of producing 6.4 million barrels of oil each day. They provide fuel to about 35,000 service stations, some 700 airports, and more than 200 ports.

World's
MOST PROFITABLE COMPANIES

2006 profits in billions of US dollars

$39.5 B	$25.4 B	$22.3 B	$21.5 B	$21.1 B
ExxonMobil, USA	Royal Dutch Shell, Netherlands	BP, UK	Citigroup, USA	Bank of America, USA

World's
Most Valuable Brand

Coca-Cola

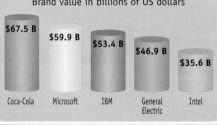

The World's
MOST VALUABLE BRANDS

Brand value in billions of US dollars

$67.5 B	$59.9 B	$53.4 B	$46.9 B	$35.6 B
Coca-Cola	Microsoft	IBM	General Electric	Intel

Coca-Cola is worth more money than any other brand in the world, with a company value of $67.5 billion. Coca-Cola is the largest nonalcoholic beverage company in the world, employing about 55,000 people. Besides soda, the company also produces water, juice, coffee, tea, and sports drinks. In fact, the company has more than 2,400 beverage products. They are ranked number one in soda and juice sales, and number two in sports drink sales. Coca-Cola products are sold in more than 200 countries.

Country That
Spends the Most on Toys

United States

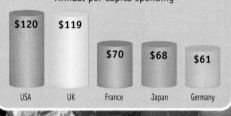

Countries That
SPEND THE MOST ON TOYS
Annual per capita spending

USA	UK	France	Japan	Germany
$120	$119	$70	$68	$61

The toy industry is booming in the United States. In 2006, Americans spent an amazing $34.8 billion on toys! That's equivalent to every single person in the country buying $120 worth of toys. It's not too much of a surprise considering toys are sold practically everywhere, from grocery stores to hardware stores. Amazingly, November and December account for about 40% of the total toy sales for the year. The United States also leads the world in toy development, marketing, and advertising, and employs more than 32,000 people in those fields.

World's
Best-Selling Candy Brand

M&M's

M&M's are the most popular candy brand in the world, accounting for about 2.13% of all sales. M&M's were first sold in the United States in 1941. Fourteen years later, peanut M&M's were introduced. In 1980, the candy-coated chocolate entered 16 countries in the international market, including Belgium, Hong Kong, Germany, Japan, and Spain. In 1981, M&M's became the first candy to travel into space. In 2002, candy lovers in more than 200 countries voted to temporarily include purple as an M&M's color.

The World's
BEST-SELLING CANDY BRANDS
Percentage of global market

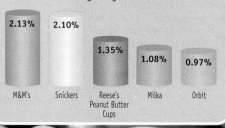

M&M's	Snickers	Reese's Peanut Butter Cups	Milka	Orbit
2.13%	2.10%	1.35%	1.08%	0.97%

World's Largest International Food Franchise

McDonald's

Serving customers in 119 different countries, there are more than 30,800 McDonald's restaurants in the world. The company adds approximately 100 new franchises each year. About 70% of the restaurant franchises are run by local businesspeople. McDonald's serves about 50 million customers each day, about 24 million of whom are in the United States. Out of respect for local cultures, restaurants in different countries modify their menus according to religious or cultural traditions. For example, there is a kosher McDonald's in Jerusalem, and the Big Macs in India are made with lamb instead of beef.

The World's
LARGEST INTERNATIONAL FOOD FRANCHISES

Number of franchises

McDonald's	Subway	KFC	Pizza Hut	Burger King
30,823	26,873	13,433	12,282	11,023

World's
Ratchest Woman

Lilianne Bettencourt

Liliane Bettencourt is the richest woman in the world with $20.7 billion. She is the only daughter of Eugene Schueller, founder of the cosmetic giant L'Oréal. In 1957, Bettencourt inherited her father's money, in addition to a controlling stake in the business. Today, L'Oréal is one of the world's most profitable cosmetics companies. A native of France, Bettencourt is the country's second-richest citizen. She has founded the Bettencourt Schueller Foundation, which grants European scientists $300,000 for research in biology or medicine.

The World's
RICHEST WOMEN

Assets in billions of US dollars

$20.7 B	$16.7 B	$16.6 B	$16.4 B	$13.0 B
Lilianne Bettencourt, France	Christy Walton, USA	Alice L. Walton, USA	Helen R. Walton, USA	Abigail Johnson, USA

World's Richest Man

Bill Gates

Bill Gates is probably one of the world's most recognizable businesspeople. He is the co-founder of Microsoft—the most valuable computer software company in the world—and he is worth an incredible $56.0 billion. As Microsoft's largest individual shareholder, Gates became a billionaire on paper when the company went public in 1986. Gates has also combined his love of art and computers to create Corbis—a successful digital image archiving company. He has been very generous with his fortune. Through his Gates Foundation, he has donated billions of dollars to health research, libraries, and education.

The World's
RICHEST MEN

Assets in billions of US dollars

$56 B	$52 B	$49 B	$33 B	$32 B
Bill Gates, USA	Warren Buffet, USA	Carlos Slim Helú, Mexico	Ingvar Kamprad, Sweden	Lakshmi Mittal, India

World's
Poorest Countries

Malawi and Somalia

Malawi and Somalia are the poorest countries in the world, with gross domestic products of just $600. Malawi is a landlocked country located in southeastern Africa, and depends on agriculture for income. However, the country's chief crop is tobacco, and cigarette consumption has decreased in recent years. Somalia—also located in eastern Africa—has suffered under the lack of government since 1991. Agriculture is the biggest part of the country's income, and trading bans on livestock have hurt the economy. The country has also suffered from natural disasters, including a destructive tsunami in late 2004.

The World's
POOREST COUNTRIES

Gross domestic product per capita in US dollars*

$600	$600	$700	$700	$800
Malawi	Somalia	Burundi	Tanzania	Democratic Republic of Congo

*Calculated by dividing the annual worth of all the goods and services produced in a country by the country's population.

World's
Richest Country

Luxembourg

Located in western Europe, the very small country of Luxembourg has a population of 474,400. It has a gross domestic product of $65,900 per person. Luxembourg's low inflation and low unemployment rates help to keep the economy solid. Industry makes up a large part of the country's gross domestic product and includes products such as iron and steel, chemicals, metal products, tires, glass, and aluminum. The country's banking community also plays a significant role in the economy, accounting for about 28% of the gross domestic product.

The World's
RICHEST COUNTRIES

Gross domestic product per capita in US dollars*

Luxembourg	United Arab Emirates	Norway	USA	Iceland
$65,900	$45,200	$42,800	$41,800	$35,700

*Calculated by dividing the annual worth of all the goods and services produced in a country by the country's population.

World's Youngest Billionaire

Athina Onassis Roussel

Greek shipping tycoon Aristotle Onassis left his granddaughter well provided for. When Athina Onassis Roussel turned 18 years old in 2003, she inherited an estimated $2.7 billion in properties, including an island in the Ionian Sea, companies, artwork, and a private jet. At 21, she became president of the Athens-based Onassis Foundation and received another $2 billion. She became the only heir to the Onassis shipping fortune when her mother, Christina, died in 1988. Currently, the estate is being managed by financial advisers. Athina married Brazilian professional equestrian show jumper Alvaro de Miranda Neto in December 2005 and the newlyweds reside in Brazil.

The World's
YOUNGEST BILLIONAIRES

Age in 2008

Athina Onassis Roussel	Hind Hariri	Albert von Thurn und Taxis	Fahd Hariri	Ayman Hariri
23	24	24	27	29

World's
Most Expensive Hotel

Hotel Martinez

The World's
MOST EXPENSIVE HOTELS

Price per night

$37,200	$35,000	$34,088	$27,277	$25,000
Hotel Martinez, France	President Wilson Hotel, Switzerland	Grand Resort Lagonissi, Greece	Hotel Cala di Volpe, Italy	Bridge Suite at Atlantis, Bahamas

The penthouse suite at the Hotel Martinez in Cannes, France, can be rented for $37,200 a night. That's more than the price of the average new car! The super-expensive suite is located on the seventh floor of the hotel and has four bedrooms that overlook the Mediterranean. In the 2,000-square-foot (186-sq-m) suite, guests can enjoy several living rooms with plasma televisions and four marble bathrooms. There is also a huge terrace with a spa Jacuzzi. The hotel is very popular with celebrities, especially when the international film festival takes place each May.

World's Most Expensive Watch

Vacheron Constantin Tour de l'Ile

With a ticket price of $1.5 million, the Tour de l'Ile watch is the most valuable watch in the world. It was created by Vacheron Constantin—the world's oldest watchmaker. The piece was made to mark the watchmaker's 250th anniversary. It took seven years to develop the watch, and an additional three years to assemble it. The watch has 834 separate parts, making it the world's most complicated timepiece. Some of the features of the Tour de l'Ile include a perpetual calendar, a moon-phase chart, a sky chart, and the sunrise and sunset times. Only seven of these luxury watches were made.

The World's MOST EXPENSIVE WATCHES

Price

$1.5 M	$839,000	$532,000	$477,000	$450,000
Tour de l'Ile	Blancpain 1735	Girard-Perregaux Opera Three	Parmigiani Fleurier Toric Corrector Quantième Perpétual	Roger Dubuis Excalibur EX 08

United States' Most Valuable Movie Franchise

Star Wars

The United States'
MOST VALUABLE MOVIE FRANCHISES

Lifetime domestic gross,
in billions of dollars adjusted for inflation

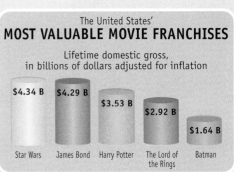

$4.34 B	$4.29 B	$3.53 B	$2.92 B	$1.64 B
Star Wars	James Bond	Harry Potter	The Lord of the Rings	Batman

The Star Wars movie franchise is the most valuable in the United States, with a combined domestic gross of $4.34 billion. Of the six movies in the franchise, *Star Wars* has brought in the most money with $797 million. Combined, the Star Wars movies have sold a total of more than 700 million tickets. Written, produced, and directed by George Lucas, the first Star Wars movie opened in 1977. Some of the movies' biggest stars include Harrison Ford, Liam Neeson, Samuel L. Jackson, Natalie Portman, and Ewan McGregor.

World's
Most Expensive Restaurant

Aragawa

With an average meal price of $277 per person, diners at Aragawa in Tokyo, Japan, had better bring their wallets! The restaurant was the country's first steak house, and it is famous for its Kobe beef. The Sumiyaki (charcoal-broiled steak) is served only with pepper and mustard, and is one of the most popular dishes at Aragawa. The formal restaurant is decorated with dark wood paneling and a sparkling chandelier to create a special atmosphere for guests.

The World's
MOST EXPENSIVE RESTAURANTS

Average cost of a meal

Aragawa, Tokyo	Eigensinn Farm, Toronto	Arpège, Paris	Sketch, London	Alain Ducasse, New York
$277	$213	$211	$176	$175

World's
Most Valuable Baseball

Mark McGwire's 70th Home-Run Baseball

Mark McGwire's 70th home-run baseball fetched $3.05 million at auction in January 1999. The bid, which was actually $2.7 million plus a large commission fee, is the most money paid for a sports artifact. The ball was only expected to sell for about $1 million. Businessman and baseball fan Todd McFarlane said he bought the ball because he wanted to own a piece of history. This famous baseball marked the end of the exciting 1998 home run race between Mark McGwire and Sammy Sosa. Both beat Roger Maris's three-decade record of 61—Sosa with 66 and McGwire with 70.

The World's
MOST VALUABLE BASEBALLS

Price paid at auction, in US dollars

$3.05 M	$517,500	$150,000	$125,500	$106,600
McGwire's 70th Home-Run Baseball	Bonds' 73rd Home-Run Baseball	Sosa's 66th Home-Run Baseball	Ruth's First Yankee Stadium Home-Run Baseball	Cub's 2003 Play-offs Foul Ball

World's
Most Valuable Production Car

Bugatti Veyron 16.4

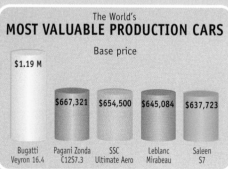

The World's
MOST VALUABLE PRODUCTION CARS

Base price

$1.19 M

| $667,321 | $654,500 | $645,084 | $637,723 |

| Bugatti Veyron 16.4 | Pagani Zonda C12S7.3 | SSC Ultimate Aero | Leblanc Mirabeau | Saleen S7 |

The Bugatti Veyron 16.4 has a hefty price tag, costing almost $1.2 million. The Veyron has a quad-turbocharged W16 engine—the equivalent of two V8 engines. The super sports car can reach a top speed of 253 miles (406 km) per hour, and can accelerate from 0 to 60 miles per hour in less than 3 seconds. Driving at full throttle, the Veyron would run out of fuel in just 12 minutes. The car debuted in October 2005, and only 70 cars are built each year. Some famous owners include Tom Cruise and Ralph Lauren.

Science Records

Computers • Technology • Solar System
Space • Video Games • Vehicles

World's
Most-Visited Web Site

Yahoo!

The Web Sites with the
MOST VISITORS

Number of new users each month, in millions

128.1 M	120.3 M	119.2 M	108.5 M	76.0 M
Yahoo!	MSN	Time Warner Network	Google	eBay

Each month, approximately 128.1 million different people visit the Yahoo! Web site. Yahoo! was founded by Stanford students David Filo and Jerry Yang in 1994, and has grown to become the world's largest global online network. In addition to being a popular search engine, Yahoo! also offers e-mail, instant messaging, information and gaming pages, as well as shopping and auction sites. Yahoo! is offered in 15 different languages and has offices in Europe, Asia Pacific, Latin America, Canada, and the United States.

Country with the
Most Internet Users

United States

The number of Internet users has doubled in the last five years. Americans now account for 20% of users worldwide. In the United States, more than 203 million people are surfing the World Wide Web. That's more than 50% of the population. Throughout the nation, the largest number of Internet users are women between the ages of 18 and 54, closely followed by men in that age group. Teens ages 12 to 17 are the third-largest Internet-using group. The average Internet user spends about 13.5 hours online per week.

The Countries with the
MOST INTERNET USERS

Users in millions

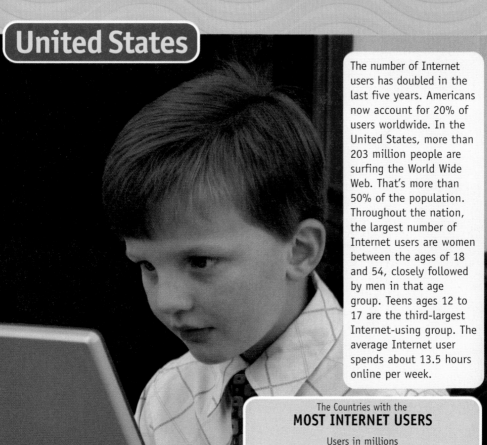

USA	China	Japan	India	Germany
203.6 M	132.0 M	88.9 M	51.0 M	47.1 M

World's Fastest Computer

BlueGene

BlueGene is the most powerful supercomputer in the world and is capable of performing 280.6 trillion calculations per second. That's about the same as every person in the world doing 40,000 calculations in a second. Housed in the Lawrence Livermore National Laboratory in California, BlueGene is made up of 131,000 processors and is two and a half times faster than the next-fastest computer. BlueGene is used by the government to study classified information.

The World's
FASTEST COMPUTERS

Calculations per second, in trillions

BlueGene	Red Storm	BGW	ASC Purple	Mare Nostrum
280.6 T	101.4 T	91.3 T	63.4 T	62.6 T

World's Most-Visited Shopping Site

eBay

When online shoppers are looking to spend money, the majority check eBay first. With 76 million visitors each month, eBay truly is the World's Online Marketplace®. The company was founded in 1995, and the online auction and shopping Web site attracts sellers and bidders from all over the world. Each year, millions of items—including spectacular treasures, unusual services, and even worthless junk—trade hands. Some of the most expensive sales include a Grumman Gulfstream II Jet for $4.9 million and a 1909 Honus Wagner baseball card for $1.65 million.

The World's MOST-VISITED SHOPPING SITES

Visitors who visited at least once during June 2006, in millions

eBay.com	Amazon.com	Walmart.com	Target.com	Shopping.com
76.0 M	48.4 M	24.5 M	23.5 M	20.2 M

Country with the
Highest Internet Use

Iceland

Iceland rates number one in Internet usage, with 86.8% of its citizens surfing the Web. That means that about 259,900 Icelandic people log on to the Internet. The Internet was first available in Iceland in 1986, and connections grew steadily each year. Approximately 84% of Internet users log on at least once a week. And 9 out of 10 individuals ages 16 to 74 are computer and Internet users. Approximately 45,000 households have broadband Internet connections. The most popular online activity in Iceland is shopping.

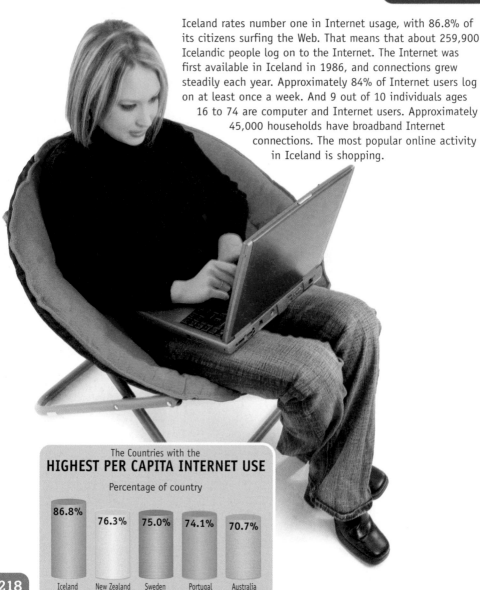

The Countries with the
HIGHEST PER CAPITA INTERNET USE
Percentage of country

Iceland	New Zealand	Sweden	Portugal	Australia
86.8%	76.3%	75.0%	74.1%	70.7%

Country with the
Most Web Sites

United States

The United States has the most sites on the World Wide Web with 54.6 million. That's more than half of the 100 million Web sites worldwide that make up the Internet today. There are currently more than 5,000 times more Web sites running today than were on the Web just 10 years ago. Web site production has increased at this incredible rate because sites have become so much easier to create. Bloggers and small business owners account for the largest percentage of new Web sites.

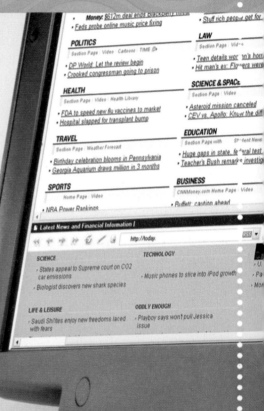

The Countries with the
MOST WEB SITES

Web sites, in millions

USA	Germany	UK	Canada	France
54.64 M	15.02 M	6.18 M	2.81 M	2.55 M

Country with the
Most Cell Phone Accounts

Luxembourg

Almost the entire population of Luxembourg is taking advantage of wireless communication, with 138 cell phone accounts per every 100 people. Many people have more than one cell phone account. Luxembourg's healthy economy and growing business and financial sectors thrive on the ability to communicate instantly. SES Global—the world's largest satellite company— is located in Luxembourg and provides cell phone services to more than 100 million people throughout Europe.

The Countries with the
MOST CELL PHONE ACCOUNTS

Cell phone accounts per 100 people

Luxembourg	Italy	Iceland	Czech Republic	Israel
138.2	108.5	108.2	105.6	105.3

Country with the
Most Cell Phone Subscribers

United States

More than 201 million people in the United States subscribe to cell phone service. That's about 62% of the country's population, and about 14% of total cell phone subscribers worldwide. As cell phone service improves and the costs go down, more and more Americans are abandoning traditional landlines in favor of wireless communication. And with the wide range of services offered by cell phone companies—including text and photo messaging, Internet accessibility, and standard voice service—many Americans rely on their phones to plan and manage their social and business schedules. Each year, cell phone sales and service totals about $12 billion.

The Countries with the
MOST CELL PHONE SUBSCRIBERS

Subscribers, in millions

United States	Russia	Japan	Germany	Italy
201.7 M	120.0 M	94.7 M	79.2 M	72.2 M

Country That
Watches the Most TV

United States and United Kingdom

People in the United States and the United Kingdom average 28 hours in front of the television each week. That means that viewers are spending a total of 1,456 hours—or 61 days—a year channel surfing. In the United States, men aged 55 and over log the most time in front of the tube each week with 40.3 hours. Children aged 6 to 11 spend the fewest, with 20.5 hours.

In the UK, television sets are in 98% of all homes, and watching shows together is a favorite family activity.

The Countries that
WATCH THE MOST TV

Average TV viewing, in hours per week

United States	United Kingdom	Italy	France	Germany
28	28	27	23	23

Planet with the Most Moons

Jupiter

Jupiter—the fifth planet from the Sun—has 63 moons. Most of these moons—also called satellites—do not resemble traditional moons. Most are quite small, measuring from just .62 miles (.99 km) to 4 miles (6.4 km) across. Jupiter's four largest moons are Ganymede, Europa, Io, and Callisto. The moons travel in an elliptical, or egg-shaped, orbit in the opposite direction that Jupiter rotates. Astronomers believe these irregular moons formed somewhere else in the solar system and were pulled into Jupiter's atmosphere when they passed too close to the planet. Astronomers are constantly finding new moons for several of the planets, partly because of the highly-sensitive telescopes and cameras now available to them.

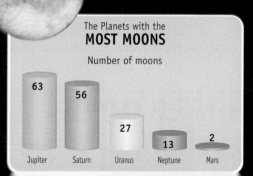

The Planets with the
MOST MOONS

Number of moons

Jupiter	Saturn	Uranus	Neptune	Mars
63	56	27	13	2

Star That Is Closest to Earth

Proxima Centauri

Proxima Centauri is approximately 24.7925 trillion miles (39.9233 trillion km) from Earth, making it our closest star other than the Sun. Light from the star reaches Earth in just 4.2 years. It is the third member of the Alpha Centauri triple system. This tiny red dwarf star is about 10% of the Sun's mass and .006% as bright. The surface temperature is thought to be about 3,000° Fahrenheit (1,650° C). More accurate measures of the star's size are not possible because it is so small. But these measurements are enough to cause scientists to believe that Proxima Centauri does not have any planets orbiting it that support life. If planets did exist, they would be too cold and dark for life-forms to exist.

The Stars that are CLOSEST TO EARTH

Distance in trillions of miles/kilometers

Proxima Centauri	Alpha Centauri	Barnard's Star	Wolf 359	Lalande 21185
24.8 T mi. 39.9 T km.	25.6 T mi. 41.2 T km.	35.1 T mi. 56.6 T km.	45.5 T mi. 73.3 T km.	48.3 T mi. 77.8 T km.

Planet with the Hottest Surface

Venus

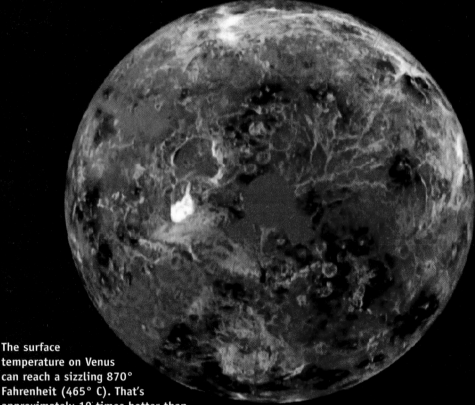

The surface temperature on Venus can reach a sizzling 870° Fahrenheit (465° C). That's approximately 19 times hotter than the average temperature on Earth. About every 19 months, Venus is closer to Earth than any other planet in the solar system. Venus is covered by a dense atmosphere. There are clouds made of acid, hurricane-strength winds, and lots of lightning. This makes it difficult to know what features are on its surface. The atmosphere also reflects a great deal of sunlight. At times, Venus is the third-brightest object in the sky, after the Sun and the Moon.

The Solar System's HOTTEST PLANETS

Average daytime temperature in degrees Fahrenheit/Celsius

Venus	Mercury	Earth	Mars	Jupiter
870°F 465°C	725°F 385°C	68°F 20°C	-76°F -60°C	-160°F -107°C

225

Planet with the Fastest Orbit

Mercury

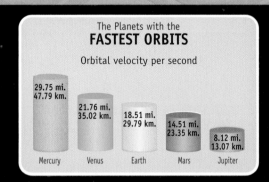

The Planets with the
FASTEST ORBITS

Orbital velocity per second

- Mercury: 29.75 mi. 47.79 km.
- Venus: 21.76 mi. 35.02 km.
- Earth: 18.51 mi. 29.79 km.
- Mars: 14.51 mi. 23.35 km.
- Jupiter: 8.12 mi. 13.07 km.

Mercury orbits the Sun at about 30 miles (48 km) per second. At this astonishing speed, the planet can circle the Sun in about 88 Earth days. On Mercury, a solar day (the time from one sunrise to the next) lasts about 176 Earth days. Mercury's surface resembles that of the Earth's moon, with flat plains, steep cliffs, and craters. Even though Mercury is the closest planet to the Sun, the temperature on the planet can change drastically. During the day, it can reach as high as 840° Fahrenheit (448° C), but at night, temperatures can fall to around -300° Fahrenheit (-184° C)!

Solar System's
Largest Planet

Jupiter

Jupiter has a radius of 43,441 miles (69,912 km)—that's almost 11 times larger than Earth's radius. In fact, the Earth could fit inside Jupiter more than 1,000 times! Jupiter is about 480 million miles (772 million km) from the Sun. It takes almost 12 Earth years for Jupiter to make one complete circle around the Sun. Although it is very large, Jupiter has a high rotation speed. One Jupiter day is less than 10 Earth hours long. That is the shortest solar day in the solar system.

The Solar System's
LARGEST PLANETS

Mean radius in miles/kilometers

Planet	Mean radius
Jupiter	43,441 mi. / 69,912 km.
Saturn	36,184 mi. / 58,232 km.
Uranus	15,759 mi. / 25,361 km.
Neptune	15,301 mi. / 24,624 km.
Earth	3,959 mi. / 6,371 km.

Planet with the Most Rings

Saturn

Scientists estimate that approximately 1,000 rings circle Saturn—hundreds more than any other planet. This ring system is only about 328 feet (100 m) thick, but reaches a diameter of 167,780 miles (270,015 km). The three major rings around the planet are named A, B, and C. Although they appear solid, Saturn's rings are made of particles of planet and satellite matter that range in size from about 1 to 15 feet (0.3 to 4.5 m). Because of the rings' brightness, scientists believe they are not as old as the planet they circle. Saturn, which is the sixth planet from the Sun, is the solar system's second-largest planet in size and mass.

The Planets
WITH THE MOST RINGS

Number of rings

Saturn	Uranus	Neptune	Jupiter
1,000	11	6	1

Planet with the
Largest Moon

Jupiter

Ganymede is the largest moon of both Jupiter and the solar system. It has a radius of 1,635 miles (2,631 km) and a diameter of 3,270 miles (5,262 km). That is almost 2.5 times larger than Earth's moon. The moon is approximately 1.4 million miles (2.25 million km) away from Jupiter and has an orbital period of about seven days. It is probably made up mostly of rock and ice. It also has lava flows, mountains, and valleys. Many of the moon's large craters were caused by collisions with comets. Ganymede has both light and dark areas that give it a textured appearance. Ganymede was discovered by Galileo Galilei and Simon Marius almost 400 years ago.

The Planets with the
LARGEST MOONS

Diameter in miles/kilometers

Ganymede	Titan	Callisto	Io	Moon
3,270 mi. 5,262 km.	3,200 mi. 5,150 km.	2,995 mi. 4,820 km.	2,264 mi. 3,643 km.	2,160 mi. 3,476 km.

Solar System's
Brightest Planet

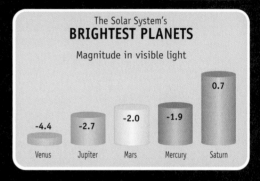

Venus

Venus is the brightest planet visible from Earth at night with a magnitude of -4.4. The planet can often be seen by the naked eye, or with a pair of binoculars. Venus appears so bright to sky gazers because it is the closest planet to Earth, and its thick clouds reflect the Sun's light. But because of this cloud cover, a simple telescope cannot reveal the planet's features. The geography of Venus consists mainly of huge plains, lowlands, and highlands.

The Solar System's
BRIGHTEST PLANETS

Magnitude in visible light

Venus	Jupiter	Mars	Mercury	Saturn
-4.4	-2.7	-2.0	-1.9	0.7

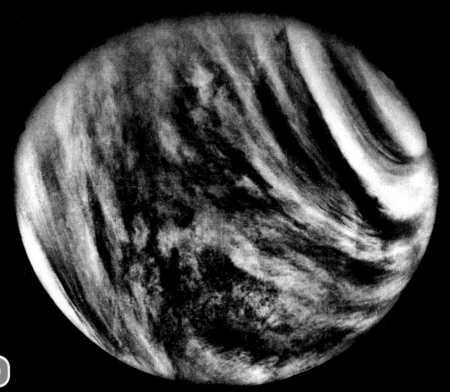

World's
Brightest Galaxy

Large Magellanic Cloud

The Large Magellanic Cloud (LMC) is the brightest galaxy in the universe with an apparent magnitude of 0.91. First noted by the explorer Ferdinand Magellan in 1519, the LMC is a small galaxy in the southern constellations. Approximately 160,000 light-years from Earth, the LMC is an irregular dwarf galaxy that orbits the Milky Way. It is full of gas and dust, and new stars are continually forming within it. It is approximately one-twentieth the size of Earth's galaxy and contains about one-tenth the number of stars.

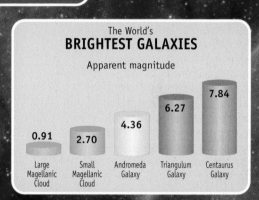

The World's
BRIGHTEST GALAXIES

Apparent magnitude

0.91	2.70	4.36	6.27	7.84
Large Magellanic Cloud	Small Magellanic Cloud	Andromeda Galaxy	Triangulum Galaxy	Centaurus Galaxy

Planet with the Longest Day

Mercury

One day on Mercury—from sunrise to sunset—lasts for 4,223.56 hours. That's equal to 176 Earth days! Mercury's unique orbit is responsible for the extra-long day. Mercury is the fastest-moving planet, traveling around the Sun once every 88 Earth days. Mercury is the smallest planet in the solar system, and it is the closest one to the sun. Because the planet is moving so quickly around the Sun, but spinning so slowly on its axis, it takes almost half an Earth year for a Mercury day to pass.

The Planets with the
LONGEST DAYS

Length of day, in hours

Mercury	Venus	Mars	Earth	Uranus
4,223.56	2,802.00	24.03	24.00	17.01

World's
Longest Space Walk

Susan Helms and James Voss

The World's
LONGEST SPACE WALKS

Length of space walk, in hours and minutes

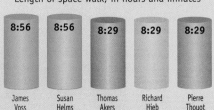

8:56	8:56	8:29	8:29	8:29
James Voss	Susan Helms	Thomas Akers	Richard Hieb	Pierre Thouot

Susan Helms and James Voss each completed a space walk that lasted 8 hours and 56 minutes on March 11, 2001. The two astronauts spent the time working on the International Space Station. They prepped a shuttle docking tunnel which needed to be moved to make room for a cargo carrier. The astronauts also attached a mounting platform that would eventually support the station's robotic arm. And even though the space walk was the longest in NASA history, the astronauts could not perform some maintenance and it was rescheduled for a future mission.

Galaxy
Closest to Earth

Canis Major Dwarf

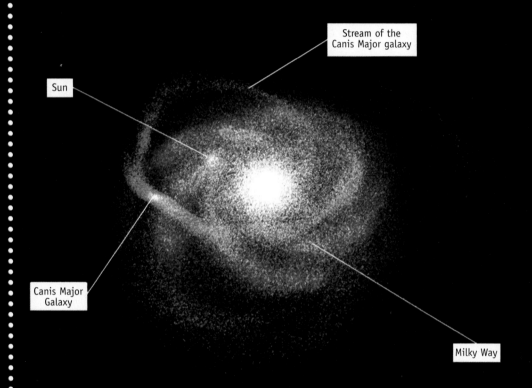

Stream of the
Canis Major galaxy

Sun

Canis Major
Galaxy

Milky Way

The Canis Major Dwarf Galaxy is the Milky Way's closest neighbor, located just 42,000 light-years from Earth. The small galaxy was just discovered by astronomers from France, Italy, the UK, and Australia in 2003. The astronomers used infrared light to see past the dust in the Milky Way. This study picked up the galaxy's cool, red stars that shine brightly in infrared light. Astronomers believe that the Canis Major Dwarf is gradually being ripped apart by the Milky Way's gravitational pull.

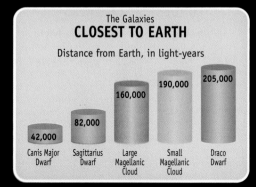

The Galaxies
CLOSEST TO EARTH

Distance from Earth, in light-years

Canis Major Dwarf	Sagittarius Dwarf	Large Magellanic Cloud	Small Magellanic Cloud	Draco Dwarf
42,000	82,000	160,000	190,000	205,000

234

World's
Best-Selling Video Game Ever

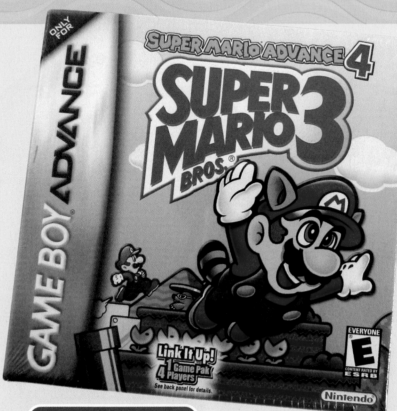

Super Mario Bros.™ 3

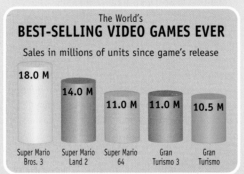

The World's
BEST-SELLING VIDEO GAMES EVER

Sales in millions of units since game's release

18.0 M	14.0 M	11.0 M	11.0 M	10.5 M
Super Mario Bros. 3	Super Mario Land 2	Super Mario 64	Gran Turismo 3	Gran Turismo

Since its release in Japan in 1988, Super Mario Bros. 3 has sold more than 18 million copies around the world. The game, which was created by Nintendo, was later released in the United States in 1990 and in Europe in 1991. Similar to the first two games in the series, players help Mario and Luigi battle King Bowser to win magic wands and save Princess Toadstool. But this version gave the game's hero special powers when he put on the raccoon, frog, or tanooki suits. It was directed by Shigeru Miyamoto, and the music was composed by Koji Kondo.

World's
Fastest Production Motorcycle

Suzuki GSX1300R Hayabusa

The World's
FASTEST PRODUCTION MOTORCYCLES

Maximum miles/kilometers per hour

186 mph 299 kph	185 mph 297 kph	181 mph 291 kph	180 mph 289 kph	173 mph 278 kph
Suzuki GSX1300R Hayabusa	Kawasaki ZX-14 Ninja	Honda CBR1100XX	Harris Yamaha YLR500	Kawasaki ZZ-R1200

This sleek speed machine, which is named after one of the world's fastest birds, is able to reach a maximum speed of 186 miles (299 km) per hour. That's about three times faster than the speed limit on most major highways. The 2006 Hayabusa features a 1299-cc, liquid-cooled DOHC engine. Its aerodynamic shape, four-cylinder engine, and six-speed transmission make the bike very popular with motorcycle enthusiasts. In 2001, motorcycle manufacturers set a guideline stating that no new production motorcycles will have a top speed above 186 miles (299 km) per hour, for safety reasons.

World's
Fastest Land Vehicle

Thrust SSC

The Vehicles with the
FASTEST SPEEDS ON LAND

Speed in miles/kilometers per hour

763 mph 1,228 kph	633 mph 1,019 kph	622 mph 1,001 kph	600 mph 966 kph	576 mph 927 kph
Thrust SSC, 1997	Thrust 2, 1983	Blue Flame, 1970	Spirit of America, 1965	Green Monster, 1965

The Thrust SSC, which stands for supersonic car, reached a speed of 763 miles (1,228 km) per hour on October 15, 1997. At that speed, a car could make it from San Francisco to New York City in less than 4 hours. The Thrust SSC is propelled by two jet engines capable of 110,000 horsepower. It has the same power as 1,000 Ford Escorts or 145 Formula One race cars. The Thrust SSC runs on jet fuel, using about 5 gallons (19 l) per second. It only takes approximately five seconds for this supersonic car to reach its top speed. It is 54 feet (16.5 m) long and weighs 7 tons (6.4 t).

World's
Fastest Passenger Train

MagLev

The superspeedy MagLev train in China carries passengers from Pudong financial district to Pudong International Airport at an average speed of 243 miles (391 km) per hour. The train reaches a top speed of 267 miles (430 km) per hour about 4 minutes into the trip. The 8-minute train ride replaces a 45-minute car trip. The MagLev, which is short for magnet levitation, actually floats in the air just above the track. Tiny magnets are used to suspend the train, and larger ones are used to pull it forward. The German-built train began commercial operation in 2004.

The World's
FASTEST PASSENGER TRAINS

Average speed in miles/kilometers per hour

Maglev, China	Eurostar, UK	Nozomi, Japan	TGV, France	Acela Express, USA
243.0 mph 391.2 kph	186.0 mph 299.3 kph	162.6 mph 261.7 kph	158.0 mph 254.3 kph	150.0 mph 241.4 kph

MLU 002N

World's
Fastest Production Car

Bugatti Veyron

The World's
FASTEST PRODUCTION CARS
Maximum miles/kilometers per hour

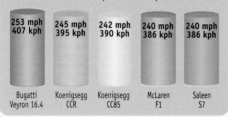

253 mph 407 kph	245 mph 395 kph	242 mph 390 kph	240 mph 386 kph	240 mph 386 kph
Bugatti Veyron 16.4	Koenigsegg CCR	Koenigsegg CC85	McLaren F1	Saleen S7

The Volkswagen Bugatti Veyron 16.4 can cruise along at a top speed of 253 miles (407 km) per hour. In fact, it can reach 62 miles (100 km) per hour in just 2 seconds, and accelerate to 186 miles (300 km) per hour in only 14 seconds. That's faster than a Formula One race car! The seven-speed semi-manual transmission takes less than a quarter of a second to change gears. The Bugatti Veyron is powered by an 8.0-liter W-16 engine. This ultimate sports car sells for about $1.2 million, and only 300 of them will be produced. Buyers can also opt to jazz up their new Veyron by adding two one-carat diamonds to the speedometer.

EB 18/4 "Veyron"

World's Largest Cruise Ship

Queen Mary 2

The World's
LARGEST CRUISE SHIPS

Length

1,132 ft. 345 m.	1,112 ft. 339 m.	1,112 ft. 339 m.	1,020 ft. 311 m.	1,020 ft. 311 m.
Queen Mary 2	Freedom of the Seas	Liberty of the Seas	Voyager of the Seas	Adventure of the Seas

The *Queen Mary 2* measures 1,132 feet (345 m) long, some 236 feet (72 m) high, and weighs 151,400 gross tons (137,320 t). This gigantic luxury ship is longer than three football fields, but can still move at a top speed of 35 miles (56 km) per hour. The $800 million ship can accommodate 2,620 passengers and 1,253 crew members. On board, guests can enjoy such amenities as the Canyon Ranch Spa, a planetarium, virtual reality golf, a disco, and the largest ballroom at sea. The *Queen Mary 2* made her maiden voyage from Southampton, England, to Fort Lauderdale, Florida, in 2004. First-class passengers paid up to $38,000 for the historic trip.

World's
Biggest Monster Truck

The Bigfoot 5 truly is a monster—it measures 15.4 feet (4.7 m) high! That's about three times the height of an average car. Bigfoot 5 has 10-foot- (3-m-) high Firestone Tundra tires each weighing 2,400 pounds (1,088 kg), giving the truck a total weight of about 38,000 pounds (17,236 kg). The giant wheels were from an arctic snow train operated in Alaska by the US Amy in the 1950s. This modified 1996 Ford F250 pickup truck is owned by Bob Chandler of St. Louis, Missouri. The great weight of this monster truck makes it too large to race.

Bigfoot 5

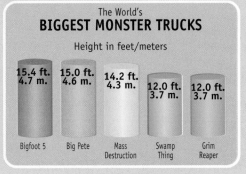

The World's
BIGGEST MONSTER TRUCKS

Height in feet/meters

15.4 ft. 4.7 m.	15.0 ft. 4.6 m.	14.2 ft. 4.3 m.	12.0 ft. 3.7 m.	12.0 ft. 3.7 m.
Bigfoot 5	Big Pete	Mass Destruction	Swamp Thing	Grim Reaper

World's
Lightest Jet

BD-5J Microjet

The BD-5J Microjet weighs only 358.8 pounds (162.7 kg), making it the lightest jet in the world. At only 12 feet (3.7 m) in length, it is one of the smallest as well. This tiny jet has a height of 5.6 feet (1.7 m) and a wingspan of 17 feet (5.2 m). The Microjet uses a TRS-18 turbojet engine. It can reach a top speed of 320 miles (514.9 km) per hour, but can only carry 32 gallons (121 l) of fuel at a time. A new BD-5J costs around $200,000. This high-tech gadget was flown by James Bond in the movie *Octopussy*, and it is also occasionally used by the U.S. military.

242

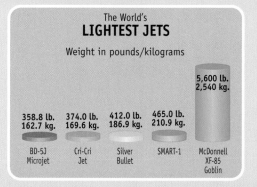

The World's
LIGHTEST JETS

Weight in pounds/kilograms

358.8 lb. 162.7 kg.	374.0 lb. 169.6 kg.	412.0 lb. 186.9 kg.	465.0 lb. 210.9 kg.	5,600 lb. 2,540 kg.
BD-5J Microjet	Cri-Cri Jet	Silver Bullet	SMART-1	McDonnell XF-85 Goblin

World's
Fastest Plane

X-43A

The World's
FASTEST PLANES

Speed in miles/kilometers per hour

7,459 mph **12,004 kph**		**1,864 mph** **3,000 kph**	**1,674 mph** **2,694 kph**	**1,540 mph** **2,478 kph**
	2,193 mph **3,529 kph**			
X-43A	Lockheed SR-71 Blackbird	MiG-25 Foxbat	Tornado	Atlas Cheetah

NASA's experimental X-43A plane reached a top speed of Mach 9.8—or more than nine times the speed of sound—on a test flight over the Pacific Ocean in November 2004. The X-43A was mounted on top of a Pegasus rocket booster and was carried into the sky by a B-52 aircraft. The booster was then fired, taking the X-43A about 110,000 feet (33,530 m) above the ground. The rocket was detached from the unmanned X-43A, and the plane flew unassisted for several minutes. At this rate of 7,459 miles (12,004 km) per hour, a plane could circle the Earth in just over three and a half hours!

World's
Fastest Roller Coaster

Kingda Ka

Kingda Ka—the newest coaster at Six Flags Great Adventure in Jackson, New Jersey—can launch riders straight up a track at a top speed of 128 miles (206 km) per hour. This hydraulic launch coaster reaches its top speed in less than 4 seconds. Kingda Ka is also the world's tallest rollercoaster at 456 feet (139 m). In addition to the horizontal rocket that starts the ride, the coaster also features a few breathtaking drops and spiral turns. The 50-second-long ride cost $25 million to build and debuted during the 2005 season.

The World's
FASTEST ROLLER COASTERS

Speed in miles per hour/kilometers per hour

128 mph 206 kph	120 mph 193 kph	106 mph 172 kph	100 mph 161 kph	100 mph 161 kph
Kingda Ka, USA	Top Thrill Dragster, USA	Dodonpa, Japan	Superman the Escape, USA	Tower of Terror, Australia

U.S. Records

Alabama to Wyoming

State with the
Oldest Mardi Gras Celebration

Alabama

The United States'
OLDEST MARDI GRAS CELEBRATIONS
Year celebration began

1831	1835	1842	1844	1867
Mobile, Alabama	New Orleans, Louisiana	Lafayette, Louisiana	Pensacola, Florida	Galveston, Texas

People in Mobile, Alabama, have been celebrating Mardi Gras since 1703, but did not have an official parade event until 1831. After a brief hiatus during the Civil War, the celebrations started back up in 1866 and have been growing ever since. Today, some 100,000 people gather in Mobile to enjoy the 22 parades that take place during the two weeks that lead up to Mardi Gras. On the biggest day—Fat Tuesday—six parades wind through the downtown waterfront, with floats and costumed dancers. But at the stroke of midnight, the partying stops and plans for next year begin.

State with the
Largest National Forest

Alaska

The United States'
LARGEST NATIONAL FORESTS

Size in square miles/kilometers

26,500 sq. mi. 68,635 sq. km.	8,433 sq. mi. 21,841 sq. km.	5,051 sq. mi. 13,082 sq. km.	4,489 sq. mi. 11,626 sq. km.	4,232 sq. mi. 10,960 sq. km.
Tongass National Forest, Alaska	Chugach National Forest, Alaska	Toiyabe National Forest, Nevada	Tonto National Forest, Arizona	Gila National Forest, New Mexico

The Tongass National Forest covers approximately 26,500 square miles (68,635 sq km) in Southeast Alaska. That's about the same size as West Virginia. It is also home to the world's largest temperate rain forest. Some of the forest's trees are more than 700 years old. About 11,000 miles (17,703 km) of shoreline are inside the park. Some of the animals that live in the forest include bears, salmon, and wolves. The world's largest concentration of bald eagles also spend the fall and winter here on the Chilkat River.

State with the Country's
Sunniest Place

Arizona

The little town of Yuma, Arizona, enjoys bright, sunny days approximately 90% of the year. That means that the sun is shining about 328 days out of each year! Yuma is located in southwestern Arizona near the borders of California and Mexico. Although the temperatures are normally in the 70s year-round, the dry desert air keeps the humidity low. And this sunny spot is drawing a crowd—Yuma is the third-fastest growing area in the United States.

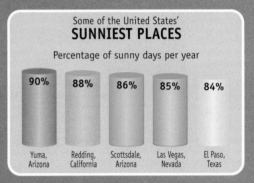

Some of the United States'
SUNNIEST PLACES

Percentage of sunny days per year

90%	88%	86%	85%	84%
Yuma, Arizona	Redding, California	Scottsdale, Arizona	Las Vegas, Nevada	El Paso, Texas

State with the
Largest Retail Headquarters

Arkansas

Wal-Mart—headquartered in Bentonville, Arkansas—logged $316.7 billion in sales in 2006. The company was founded in 1962 by Arkansas native Sam Walton, who saw his small variety stores grow into giant grocery stores, membership warehouse clubs, and deep-discount warehouse outlets. Walton's original store in Bentonville now serves as the company's visitor center. Each year, the company gives back some of what it earns—in 2006 Wal-Mart contributed $245 million to nonprofit organizations.

The United States'
LARGEST RETAIL HEADQUARTERS

2006 sales, in billions of US dollars

$316.7 B	$81.5 B	$60.6 B	$52.7 B	$43.2 B
Wal-Mart, Arkansas	The Home Depot, Georgia	Kroger, Ohio	Target, Minnesota	Lowes, North Carolina

State with the
Highest Avocado Production

California

The United States'
TOP AVOCADO PRODUCERS

Production in tons/metric tons

**270 tons
244.9 t.**

**7.9 tons
7.2 t.**

**0.5 tons
0.45 t.**

California   Florida   Hawaii

California is the country's top producer of avocados—harvesting about 270 tons (244.9 t), or 96% of the United States' crop. There are approximately 7,000 growers in the state, and each farm is around 10 acres (4.05 ha) in size. In one year, a single avocado tree can produce some 60 pounds (27.2 kg), or about 150 pieces, of fruit. Because of its warm coastal climate, the state can grow avocados year-round. The town of Fallbrook is known as the Avocado Capital of the World and hosts the annual Avocado Festival each year.

State's Baseball Team with the Highest Seasonal Attendance

Colorado

In 1993, the seasonal attendance for the Colorado Rockies was an impressive 4.48 million fans. The Rockies finished up their inaugural season in October of the same year with the most wins by a National League expansion team. The Rockies played at Mile High Stadium for their first two years. The team moved to Denver's Coors Field in 1995. The new park was designed to have 43,800 seats, but with such high attendance at Mile High Stadium, architects reworked the plans to include 50,200 seats. The team proceeded to sell out 203 consecutive games.

Baseball Teams with the
HIGHEST SEASONAL ATTENDANCE

Seasonal attendance, in millions

Colorado Rockies, 1993	New York Yankees, 2004	Los Angeles Dodgers, 2005	Los Angeles Dodgers, 2004	Atlanta Braves, 1997
4.48 M	3.77 M	3.60 M	3.48 M	3.46 M

State with the
Oldest Theme Park

Connecticut

Lake Compounce in Bristol, Connecticut, first opened as a picnic park in 1846. The park's first electric roller coaster, the Green Dragon, was introduced in 1914 and cost 10 cents per ride. It was replaced by the WildCat in 1927, and the wooden coaster still operates today. In 1996 the park got a $50 million upgrade, which included the thrilling new roller coaster Boulder Dash. It is the only coaster to be built into a mountainside. Another $3.3 million was spent on upgrades in 2005, including an 800-foot (244-m) lazy river.

The United States'
OLDEST THEME PARKS

Years of establishment

1846	1870	1878	1879	1894
Lake Compounce, Connecticut	Cedar Point, Ohio	Idlewood Park, Pennsylvania	Seabreeze Park, New Jersey	Lakemont Park, Pennsylvania

State with the Largest
Pumpkin-Throwing Contest

Delaware

Each year approximately 36,000 people gather in Sussex County, Delaware, for the annual World Championship Punkin Chunkin. More than 60 teams compete during the three-day festival to see who can chuck their pumpkin the farthest. Each team constructs a machine that has a mechanical or compressed-air firing device—no explosives are allowed. The farthest a pumpkin has traveled during the championship is 4,434 feet (1,352 m), or the length of twelve football fields. The total combined distance of all the pumpkins chunked at the 2005 championship totaled almost 10 miles (16 km). Each year the festival raises about $100,000 and benefits St. Jude Children's Hospital.

The United States'
LARGEST PUMPKIN-THROWING CONTESTS

Spectators

Millsboro, Delaware	Morton, Illinois	York, Pennsylvania	Busit, New York	Salina, Kansas
36,000	3,700	3,000	2,500	1,100

State with the
Most Lightning Strikes

Florida

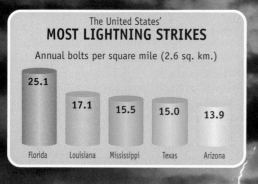

The United States'
MOST LIGHTNING STRIKES

Annual bolts per square mile (2.6 sq. km.)

Florida	Louisiana	Mississippi	Texas	Arizona
25.1	17.1	15.5	15.0	13.9

Southern Florida is known as the Lightning Capital of the United States, with 59 bolts occurring over each square mile (2.6 sq km)—the equivalent of 10 city blocks—each year. Some 70% of all strikes occur between noon and 6:00 P.M., and the most dangerous months are July and August. Most lightning bolts measure 2 to 3 miles (5.2 to 7.8 km) long and can generate between 100 million to 1 billion volts of electricity. The air in a lightning bolt is heated to 50,000 degrees Fahrenheit (27,760 degrees C).

State with the Largest
State Sports Hall of Fame

Georgia

The United States'
LARGEST SPORTS HALLS OF FAME

Square feet/square meters

Georgia Sports Hall of Fame	Alabama Sports Hall of Fame	Virginia Sports Hall of Fame	Mississippi Sports Hall of Fame	Kansas Sports Hall of Fame
43,000 sq. ft. 3,995 sq. m.	33,000 sq. ft. 3,066 sq. m.	32,000 sq. ft. 3,000 sq. m.	21,542 sq. ft. 2,001 sq. m.	20,000 sq. ft. 1,900 sq. m.

The Georgia Sports Hall of Fame fills 43,000 square feet (3,995 sq m) with memorabilia from Georgia's most accomplished prep, college, amateur, and professional athletes. Some 230,000 bricks, 245 tons (222 t) of steel, and 7,591 pounds (3,443 kg) of glass were used in its construction. The hall owns more than 3,000 artifacts and displays about 1,000 of them at a time. Some Hall of Famers include baseball legend Hank Aaron, Olympic basketball great Theresa Edwards, and Super Bowl I champion Bill Curry.

State with the Largest Submillimeter Wavelength Telescope

Hawaii

Mount Kea—located on the island of Hawaii—is the home to the world's largest submillimeter telescope with a diameter of 49 feet (15 m). The James Clerk Maxwell Telescope (JCMT) is used to study our solar system, interstellar dust and gas, and distant galaxies. Mount Kea also houses the world's largest optical/infrared (Keck I and II) and dedicated infrared (UKIRT) telescopes in the world. Mount Kea is an ideal spot for astronomy because the atmosphere above the dormant volcano is very dry with little cloud cover, and its distance from city lights ensures a dark night sky.

World's Largest
SUBMILLIMETER WAVELENGTH TELESCOPES

Diameter of lens in feet/meters

James Clerk Maxwell Telescope (JCMT), Hawaii	Caltech Submillimeter Observatory (CSO), Hawaii	Atacama Submillimeter Telescope (ASTE), Chile	Heinrich Hertz Telescope (HHT), Arizona	Submillimeter Telescope (SMT), Arizona
49 ft. 15 m.	34.0 ft. 10.4 m.	32.8 ft. 10 m.	32.8 ft. 10 m.	32.8 ft. 10 m.

State with the
Longest Main Street

Idaho

The city of Island Park, Idaho, has the country's longest main street at 33 miles (53.1 km). In the 1930s, the stretch of land ran through the city and housed several casinos that employed many residents. Laws stated that gambling could not take place outside city lines, so a businessman decided to make the entire strip of land a part of the town. The town, however, only measures about 500 feet (152.4 m) wide in some sections. Known as U.S. 20, the road is the main highway into Yellowstone National Park.

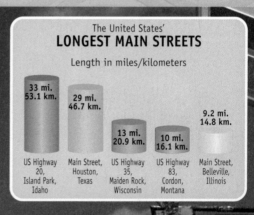

The United States'
LONGEST MAIN STREETS

Length in miles/kilometers

33 mi. 53.1 km.	29 mi. 46.7 km.	13 mi. 20.9 km.	10 mi. 16.1 km.	9.2 mi. 14.8 km.
US Highway 20, Island Park, Idaho	Main Street, Houston, Texas	US Highway 35, Maiden Rock, Wisconsin	US Highway 83, Cordon, Montana	Main Street, Belleville, Illinois

State with the
Largest Cookie Factory

Illinois

The United States'
LARGEST COOKIE FACTORIES

Area in square feet/square meters

1.75 M sq. ft. 162,000 sq. m.	500,000 sq. ft. 46,452 sq. m.	325,000 sq. ft. 30,194 sq. m.	265,000 sq. ft. 24,619 sq. m.	97,000 sq. ft. 9,012 sq. m.
Nabisco, Illinois	Entemann's, New York	Interstate Bakeries Corporation, Missouri	Pepperidge Farm, Connecticut	Otis Spunkmeyer, Texas

The Nabisco factory covers 46 acres (18.6 ha) on South Kedzie Avenue in Chicago, Illinois. The 1.75 million-square-foot (162,000-sq-m) cookie factory is also one of the largest bakeries in the world. The Nabisco plant employs about 2,000 workers, and they produce about 320 million pounds (145 million kg) of Oreo cookies, Fig Newtons, and Ritz Crackers each year. The factory has storage capacity of 8.5 million pounds (3.9 million kg) of flour, 2.4 million pounds (1.1 million kg) of sugar, and 1.5 million pounds (680,388 kg) of vegetable oil. There are also 20 ovens in the facility that measure about 300 feet (91 m) in length.

State with the Largest
Half Marathon

Indiana

Cars aren't the only things racing in Indianapolis. Each May some 35,000 runners take part in the Indianapolis Life 500 Festival Mini-Marathon. This makes the mini-marathon the nation's largest half marathon and the nation's eighth longest road race. The 13.1-mile (21.1-km) race winds through downtown and includes a lap along the Indianapolis Motor Speedway oval. About 100 musical groups entertain the runners as they complete the course. A giant pasta dinner and after-race party await the runners at the end of the day. The mini-marathon is part of a weekend celebration that centers around the Indianapolis 500 auto race.

The United States'
LARGEST HALF MARATHONS

Number of runners

35,000	25,000	24,000	20,000	18,000
Indianapolis Life 500 Festival Mini-Marathon, Indiana	County Race for the Cure, Michigan	Rock 'n' Roll Half Marathon, Arizona	Rock 'n' Roll Half Marathon, Virginia	Chicago Half Marathon, Illinois

State with the
Highest Egg Production

Iowa

The United States'
TOP EGG PRODUCERS

Number of eggs produced annually,
in billions

12.98 B	7.51 B	6.61 B	6.25 B	5.08 B
Iowa	Ohio	Pennsylvania	Indiana	California

Iowa tops all other states in the country in egg production, turning out more than 12.9 billion eggs per year. That's enough to give every person in the United States about 3 and a half dozen eggs each! That's a good thing, because each person in America eats about 256 eggs per year. The state has 45 million laying hens, and each is capable of laying about 240 eggs a year. These hungry hens eat about 42 million bushels of corn and 21 million bushels of soybeans annually. In addition to selling the eggs as is, Iowa's processing plants turn them into frozen, liquid, dried, or specialty egg products.

State with the
Windiest City

Kansas

The United States'
WINDIEST CITIES

Average wind speed

13.9 mph 22.4 kph	13.5 mph 21.7 kph	13.1 mph 21.1 kph	12.9 mph 20.8 kph	12.8 mph 20.6 kph
Dodge City, Kansas	Amarillo, Texas	Rochester, Minnesota	Lihue, Hawaii	Chester, Minnesota

According to average annual wind speeds collected by the National Climatic Data Center, Dodge City is the windiest city in the United States, with an average wind speed of 14 miles (22.5 km) per hour. Located in Ford County, the city borders the Santa Fe Trail and is rich in history. The city was established in 1872 and had a reputation as a tough cowboy town. With help from legendary sheriffs like Wyatt Earp, order was restored and the town grew steadily. Today tourists come to take in the area history.

State with the World's
Largest Fireworks Display

Kentucky

The World's
LARGEST FIREWORKS DISPLAYS

Number of fireworks shells used

60,000	35,000	22,000	12,000	10,000
Thunder Over Louisville, Kentucky	Macy's 4th of July, New York	Sailfest, Connecticut	Pops Concert at the Esplanade, Massachusetts	Central Pennsylvania 4th Fest, Pennsylvania

Thunder Over Louisville is the world's largest fireworks display, drawing approximately 800,000 spectators each year. It is the opening ceremony for the Kentucky Derby Festival. Eight 400-foot (122-m) barges line both sides of the Second Street Bridge and serve as a stage for the 26-minute show. During the show, some 60 tons (54 t) of fireworks shells and 250 tons (227 t) of launching tubes are used. The show is set to all types of music, ranging from rock and roll to Broadway tunes. Millions of people worldwide also see the show when it's rebroadcast on the 4th of July to 150 countries.

State with the
Largest Alligator Population

Louisiana

GATOR XING
NEXT 1/2 MILE

The United States'
LARGEST ALLIGATOR
POPULATIONS

Total number of alligators,
in millions/thousands

2.0 M	1.4 M	400,000	100,000	80,000
Louisiana	Florida	Texas	South Carolina	Georgia

There are approximately 2 million alligators living in Louisiana. About 1.5 million alligators live in the wild, and another half million are raised in farms. In 1986, Louisiana began an alligator ranching business, which encouraged farmers to raise thousands of the reptiles each year. The farmers must return some alligators to the wild, but they are allowed to sell the rest for profit. And, the released alligators have an excellent chance of thriving in the wild because they have been well fed and are a good size. Although alligators can be found in the state's bayous, swamps, and ponds, most live in Louisiana's 3 million acres (1.2 million ha) of coastal marshland.

State with the Oldest State Fair

Maine

The first Skowhegan State Fair took place in 1819—a year before Maine officially became a state! The fair took place in January, and hundreds of people came despite the harsh weather. Originally sponsored by the Somerset Central Agricultural Society, the fair name became official in 1842. State fairs were very important in the early 1900s. With no agricultural colleges in existence, fairs became the best way for farmers to learn about new agricultural methods and equipment. Today the Skowhegan State Fair features more than 7,000 exhibitors who compete for prize money totaling more than $200,000. The fair also includes a demolition derby, a children's barnyard, concerts, livestock exhibits, and arts and crafts.

The United States'
OLDEST STATE FAIRS
Year fair first held

1819	1820	1851	1851	1862
Skowhegan State Fair, Maine	Three County Fair, Maine	Bangor State Fair, Maine	Brooklyn Fair, Connecticut	Woodstock Fair, Vermont

State with the
Oldest Airport

Maryland

Wright brothers exhibit at
The College Park Aviation Museum

The United States'
OLDEST AIRPORTS

Year opened

1909	1911	1920	1921	1924
College Park Airport, Maryland	Robertson Airport, Connecticut	Hartness State Airport, Vermont	Bell County Airport, Kentucky	Page Field, Florida

The Wright brothers founded College Park Airport in 1909 to teach Army officers how to fly and it has been in operation ever since. The airport is now owned by the Maryland-National Capital Park and Planning Commission and is on the Register of Historic Places. Many aviation "firsts" occurred at this airport, such as the first woman passenger in the United States (1909), the first test of a bomb-dropping device (1911), and the first U.S. Air Mail Service (1918). The College Park Aviation Museum is located on the grounds and houses aviation memorabilia.

State with the
Oldest Baseball Stadium

Massachusetts

Fenway Park opened its doors to baseball fans on April 20, 1912. The Boston Red Sox—the park's home team—won the World Series that year. The park celebrated in 2004 when the Sox won the World Series again. The park is also the home of the Green Monster—a giant 37-foot (11.3-m) wall with an additional 23-foot (7-m) screen that has plagued home-run hitters since the park first opened. The park's unique dimensions were not to prevent home-runs, however. They were meant to keep nonpaying fans outside. A seat out in the right-field bleachers is painted red to mark where the longest measurable home-run hit inside the park landed. It measured 502 feet (153 m) and was hit by Ted Williams in 1946. Some of the other baseball legends who played at Fenway include Cy Young, Babe Ruth, Jimmie Fox, and Carlton Fisk.

The United States'
OLDEST BASEBALL STADIUMS
Year built

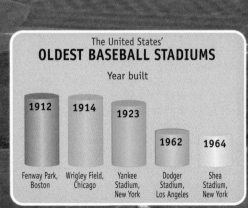

1912	1914	1923	1962	1964
Fenway Park, Boston	Wrigley Field, Chicago	Yankee Stadium, New York	Dodger Stadium, Los Angeles	Shea Stadium, New York

BOSTON RED SOX

State with the World's
Largest Indoor Waterfall

Michigan

The 114-foot (34.7-m) waterfall located in the lobby of the International Center in Detroit, Michigan, is the tallest indoor waterfall in the world. The backdrop of this impressive waterfall is a 9,000-square-foot (840-sq-m) slab of marble that was imported from the Greek island of Tinos and installed by eight marble craftsmen. About 6,000 gallons (27,276 l) of water spill down the waterfall each minute. That's the liquid equivalent of 80,000 cans of soda! Visitors can see this $1.5 million creation as they stroll through the International Center, which also houses many retail shops. Located in the historic Trappers Alley in the Greektown section of the city, the 8-story building was formerly used as a seed warehouse.

The World's Largest
INDOOR WATERFALLS

Height in feet/meters

114 ft. 34.7 m.	90 ft. 27.4 m.	85 ft. 26.1 m.	70 ft. 21.3 m.	60 ft. 18.3 m
International Center, Michigan	Trump Tower, New York	Mohegan Sun, Connecticut	Orchid Hotel, India	Casino Windsor, Michigan

State with the
Largest Indoor Theme Park

Minnesota

The Park at MOA is located inside of the Mall of America and covers 7 acres (2.8 ha). The park offers 30 rides, including the Xcel Energy Log Chute, skyscraper Ferris wheel, Timber Twister roller coaster, Mighty Axe, and the Mystery Mine Ride. Some of the other attractions at the park are a rock-climbing wall, petting zoo, and game arcade. The park is completely heated by a giant glass ceiling and the guests' body heat. Even during the cold Minnesota winter, the air conditioning is running full time.

The United States'
LARGEST INDOOR THEME PARKS
Area in acres/hectares

7 ac. 2.8 ha.	5 ac. 2.0 ha.	2.3 ac. 0.9 ha.	1.1 ac. 0.45 ha.	1 ac. 0.4 ha.
The Park at MOA, Minnesota	Adventuredome Theme Park, Nevada	DisneyQuest, Florida	Great Wolf Lodge, Kansas	The Parthenon at Mt. Olympus, Wisconsin

State with the
Most Catfish

Mississippi

There are more than 530 million catfish in Mississippi—more than 55% of the world's farm-raised supply. That's almost enough to give every person in the state 235 fish each. Mississippi's catfish crop is worth about $218 million annually. There are about 360 catfish producers farming 100,000 water acres (40,468 ha). The state's residents are quite proud of their successful fish industry and celebrate at the World Catfish Festival in Belzoni.

The States with the
MOST CATFISH

Number of catfish, in millions

State	Number
Mississippi	530 M
Louisiana	210 M
Alabama	190 M
Arkansas	125 M
Texas	70 M

State with the Largest
Outdoor Musical Theater

Missouri

The United States'
LARGEST OUTDOOR MUSICAL THEATERS

Square feet/square meters

80,000 sq. ft. 7,432 sq. m.	55,000 sq. ft. 5,100 sq. m.	45,000 sq. ft. 4,200 sq. m.	37,000 sq. ft. 3,500 sq. m.	12,000 sq. ft. 1,100 sq. m.
The Muny, Missouri	Alpine Valley Music Theater, Wisconsin	Journal Pavilion, New Mexico	Miller Outdoor Theater, Texas	Starlight Theater, Missouri

The Municipal Theatre in St. Louis—affectionately known as The Muny—is the nation's largest outdoor theater, with 80,000 square feet (7,432 sq m) and 11,500 seats—about the same size as a regulation soccer field. Amazingly, construction on the giant theater was completed in just 42 days at a cost of $10,000. The theater opened in 1917 with a production of Verdi's *Aïda*, and the best seats cost only $1.00. Today, The Muny offers classic Broadway shows each summer, with past productions including *Aïda*, *The King and I*, *The Wizard of Oz*, and *Oliver!* And the last nine rows of the theater are always held as free seats for the public, just as they have been since The Muny opened.

State with the
Largest County Park

Montana

The United States'
LARGEST COUNTY PARKS

Size in acres/hectares

10,000 ac. 4,047 ha.	9,500 ac. 3,845 ha.	8,000 ac. 3,237 ha.	7,000 ac. 2,822 ha.	4,700 ac. 1,902 ha.
Beaver Creek Park, Montana	Grant Ranch County, California	Caspers Wilderness Park, California	Dorey Park, Virgina	Ward Pound Ridge Reservation, New York

Beaver Creek Park is the nation's largest county park with 10,000 acres (4,047 ha). Located at the base of the Bear Paw Mountains of Montana, the park measures about 1 mile (1.6 km) wide and 17 miles (27.3 km) long. Some of the most popular activities at the park include hiking, camping, cross-country skiing, and snowmobiling. Beaver Creek Park also has two large lakes that are stocked with trout for year-round fishing. Many animals also call the park home, including mule deer, bobcat, beaver, coyote, fox, mink, pheasant, grouse, golden eagle, and hawk.

State with the Largest Nocturnal Animal Exhibit

Nebraska

The Henry Doorly Zoo in Omaha, Nebraska, is home to the Kingdom of the Night exhibit, which occupies more than 42,000 square feet (3,901 sq m) of the zoo's Desert Dome. There are five different areas inside the 0.75 acre (0.3 ha) exhibit, including the canyon, the African diorama, the wet cave, the Eucalyptus forest, and the dry cave. Some of the animals featured in Kingdom of the Night include aardvarks, meerkats, Japanese giant salamander, wallabies, and bats. The zoo has reversed the daily cycle of these animals, making the exhibit light in the night and dark in the day, so the animals are most active when visitors are there.

The United States'
LARGEST NOCTURNAL ANIMAL EXHIBITS

Size in square feet/square meters

Kingdoms of the Night, Nebraska	Animals of the Night, Tennessee	Day and Night Exhibit, Washington	Masters of the Night, Texas	Frogtown USA, OH
42,000 sq. ft. 3,901 sq. m.	35,000 sq. ft. 3,252 sq. m.	20,000 sq. ft. 1,858 sq. m.	5,000 sq. ft. 465 sq. m.	600 sq. ft. 56 sq. m.

State with the World's
Largest Glass Sculpture

Nevada

The World's
LARGEST GLASS SCULPTURES

Length in feet/meters

65.7 ft. 20 m.	55 ft. 16.8 m.	49.2 ft. 15 m.	43 ft. 13.1 m.	29 ft. 8.8 m.
Fiori di Como, Nevada	The Chihuly Tower, Oklahoma	Borealis, Michigan	Fireworks of Glass, Indiana	Cobalt Blue Chandelier, Washington

Fiori di Como—the breathtaking chandelier at the Bellagio Hotel in Las Vegas, Nevada— measures 65.7 feet by 29.5 feet (20 m by 9 m). Created by Dale Chihuly, the handblown glass chandelier consists of more than 2,000 discs of colored glass. Each disc is about 18 inches (45.7 cm) wide and hangs about 20 feet (6.1 m) overhead. Together, these colorful discs look like a giant field of flowers. The chandelier required about 10,000 pounds of steel (4,536 kg) and 40,000 pounds (18,144 kg) of handblown glass. The sculpture's name translates to "Flowers of Como." The Bellagio was modeled after the hotel on Lake Como in Italy.

State with the
Oldest Post Office

The Hinsdale Post Office opened its doors in 1816, and has been in operation ever since. At that time, James Madison was the country's fourth president and the Civil War was still 45 years away. The mail was delivered by horse and wagon and there were no paved roads. In the mid 1800s, nearby Brattleboro, Vermont, was connected to the railroad and mail was moved that way. In 1905, the first rural route was in place and mail was delivered to some homes by horse and buggy. Today the historic building is equipped with modern technology, and the price of a stamp is 3100% higher than it was in 1816.

New Hampshire

The United States'
OLDEST POST OFFICES

Year established

1816	1859	1887	1892	1893
Hinsdale, New Hampshire	Galena, Illinois	Memphis, Tennessee	Brooklyn, New York	Hoboken, New Jersey

State with the World's
Longest Boardwalk

New Jersey

The World's
LONGEST BOARDWALKS
Length in miles/kilometers

4.0 mi. 6.4 km.	3.0 mi. 4.8 km.	2.5 mi. 4.0 km.	2.3 mi. 3.7 km.	2.0 mi. 3.2 km.
Atlantic City, New Jersey	Coney Island, New York	FDR Boardwalk, New York	Corkscrew Swamp Sanctuary, Florida	Jarzoo Boardwalk, Sweden

The famous boardwalk in Atlantic City, New Jersey, stretches for 4 miles (6.4 km) along the beach. Combined with the adjoining boardwalk in Ventnor, the length increases to just under 6 miles (9.7 km). The 60-foot-(18-m) wide boardwalk opened on June 26, 1870. It was the first boardwalk built in the United States, and was designed to keep sand out of the tourists' shoes. Today the boardwalk is filled with amusement parks, shops, restaurants, and hotels. The boardwalk recently recieved a $100 million face-lift, which included new roofs, signs, and storefronts to surrounding buildings. About 37 million people take a stroll along the walk each year.

State with the World's
Largest Balloon Festival

New Mexico

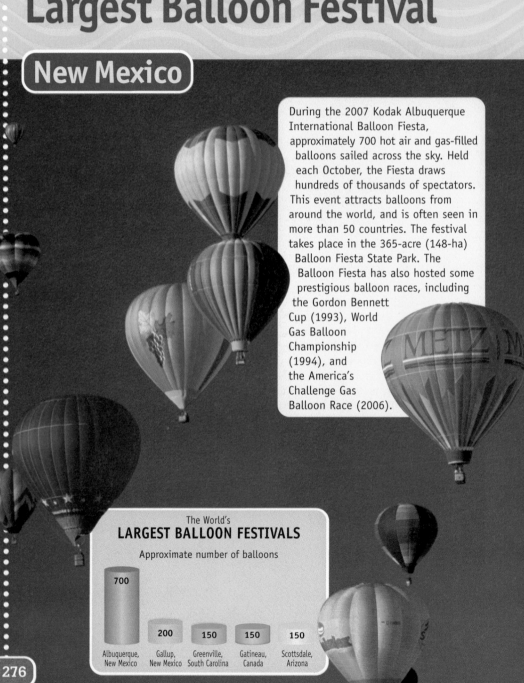

During the 2007 Kodak Albuquerque International Balloon Fiesta, approximately 700 hot air and gas-filled balloons sailed across the sky. Held each October, the Fiesta draws hundreds of thousands of spectators. This event attracts balloons from around the world, and is often seen in more than 50 countries. The festival takes place in the 365-acre (148-ha) Balloon Fiesta State Park. The Balloon Fiesta has also hosted some prestigious balloon races, including the Gordon Bennett Cup (1993), World Gas Balloon Championship (1994), and the America's Challenge Gas Balloon Race (2006).

The World's
LARGEST BALLOON FESTIVALS

Approximate number of balloons

Albuquerque, New Mexico	Gallup, New Mexico	Greenville, South Carolina	Gatineau, Canada	Scottsdale, Arizona
700	200	150	150	150

State with the
Largest Underwater Tunnel

New York

The Brooklyn-Battery Tunnel measures 1.73 miles (2.78 km) long, making it the longest underwater tunnel in North America and longest continuous underwater vehicular tunnel in the world. The tunnel passes under the East River and connects Battery Park in Manhattan with the Red Hook section of Brooklyn. It took 13,900 tons (12,609 t) of steel, about 205,000 cubic yards (156,700 cu m) of concrete, approximately 1,871 miles (3,011 km) of electrical wire, some 883,391 bolts, and 799,000 wall and ceiling tiles to build the tunnel. Completed in 1950, the $90-million tunnel carries about 60,000 vehicles a day.

The United States'
LONGEST UNDERWATER TUNNELS

Length in miles/kilometers

1.73 mi. 2.78 km.	1.70 mi. 2.73 km.	1.69 mi. 2.72 km.	1.62 mi. 2.62 km.	1.56 mi. 2.51 km.
Brooklyn-Battery Tunnel, New York	E. Johnson Memorial Tunnel, Colorado	Eisenhower Memorial Tunnel, Colorado	Holland Tunnel, New York	Lincoln Tunnel, New York

State with the
Oldest State University

North Carolina

The University of North Carolina (UNC) was founded in 1789 but did not accept its first student at Chapel Hill until February 1795 because of a lack of funding. By the following month, the university consisted of two buildings, two professors, and 41 students. This makes UNC the only university in the United States to graduate students in the 18th century. Today, the University of North Carolina's 16 campuses have more than 27,500 undergraduates and 3,100 faculty. The university offers more than 100 fields of study, and grants bachelor's, master's, and doctoral degrees.

The United States'
OLDEST PUBLIC UNIVERSITIES
Year established

University of North Carolina	University of Vermont	University of Georgia	University of South Carolina	State University of New York, New Paltz
1795	1801	1803	1803	1828

State with the
Tallest Metal Sculpture

North Dakota

The United States'
TALLEST METAL SCULPTURES

Height in feet/meters

110 ft. 33.5 m.	**70 ft. 21.3 m.**	**70 ft. 21.3 m.**	**60 ft. 18.3 m.**	**40 ft. 12.2 m.**
Geese in Flight, North Dakota	Bass Fish, North Dakota	Deer Crossing, North Dakota	Egyptian Longhorn, South Dakota	Giant Pheasant Family, North Dakota

In August 2001, Gary Greff created a 110-foot- (33.5-m-) tall metal sculpture along the stretch of road between Gladstone and Regent, North Dakota. That's the height of an 11-story building! The 154-foot- (46.9-m-) long sculpture is called *Geese in Flight*, and shows Canadian geese traveling across the prairie. Greff has created several other towering sculptures nearby, and the road has become known as the Enchanted Highway. He created these sculptures to attract tourists to the area and to support his hometown. He relies only on donations to finance his work.

279

State with the World's
Largest Twins Gathering

Ohio

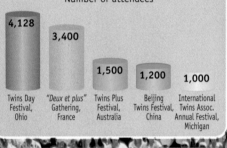

The World's
LARGEST TWINS GATHERING
Number of attendees

4,128	3,400	1,500	1,200	1,000
Twins Day Festival, Ohio	*"Deux et plus"* Gathering, France	Twins Plus Festival, Australia	Beijing Twins Festival, China	International Twins Assoc. Annual Festival, Michigan

Each August, the town of Twinsburg, Ohio, hosts more than 4,100 twins at its annual Twins Day Festival. Both identical and fraternal twins from around the world participate, and many dress alike. The twins take part in games and contests, such as the oldest identical twins and the twins with the widest combined smile. There is also a "Double Take" parade, which is nationally televised. Since twins from ages 90 to just 11 days old have attended, there are special twin programs for all age groups. The event began in 1976 in honor of Aaron and Moses Wilcox, twin brothers who inspired the city to adopt its name in 1817.

State with the World's
Longest Multiple Arch Dam

Oklahoma

With a length of 6,565 feet (2,001 m), the Pensacola Dam is the world's longest multiple arch dam. Built in 1941, the dam is located on the Grand River and contains the Lake of the Cherokees—one of the largest reservoirs of the country with 46,500 surface acres (18,818 ha) of water. The dam stands 145 feet (44 m) high. It was made out of 535,000 cubic yards of concrete, some 655,000 barrels of cement, another 10 million pounds (4.5 million kg) of structural steel, and 75,000 pounds (340,194 kg) of copper. The dam cost $27 million to complete.

The World's
LONGEST MULTIPLE ARCH DAMS

Length in feet/meters

6,565 ft. 2,001 m.	4,700 ft. 1,433 m.	4,297 ft. 1,310 m.	3,156 ft. 962 m.	800 ft. 244 m.
Pensacola Dam, Oklahoma	New Waddell Dam, Arizona	Daniel Johnson Dam, Canada	Florence Lake Dam, California	Mountain Dell Dam, Utah

State with the Deepest Lake

Oregon

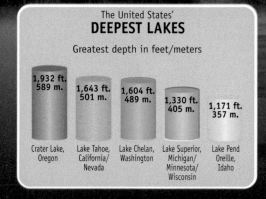

The United States'
DEEPEST LAKES

Greatest depth in feet/meters

Crater Lake, Oregon	Lake Tahoe, California/ Nevada	Lake Chelan, Washington	Lake Superior, Michigan/ Minnesota/ Wisconsin	Lake Pend Oreille, Idaho
1,932 ft. 589 m.	1,643 ft. 501 m.	1,604 ft. 489 m.	1,330 ft. 405 m.	1,171 ft. 357 m.

At a depth of 1,932 feet (589 m), Crater Lake in Southern Oregon partially fills the remains of an old volcano basin. The crater was formed almost 7,700 years ago when Mount Mazama erupted, and then collapsed. The lake averages about 5 miles (8 km) in diameter. Crater Lake National Park—the nation's fifth oldest park— surrounds the majestic lake and measures 249 square miles (645 sq km). The area's large snowfalls average 530 inches (1,346 cm) a year, and supply Crater Lake with its water. In additional to being the United States' deepest lake, it's also the eighth deepest lake in the world.

State with the
Oldest Drive-In Theater

Pennsylvania

Shankweiler's Drive-In Theater opened in 1934 and is the country's second drive-in theater, but it is the oldest one still operating today. Located in Orefield, Pennsylvania, the single-screen theater can accommodate 320 cars. Approximately 90% of the theater's guests are children. Although they originally used sound boxes located beside the cars, today patrons can tune into a special radio station to hear the movies' music and dialogue. Shankweiler's is open from April to September.

The United States'
OLDEST DRIVE-IN THEATERS

Year opened

1934	1937	1939	1943	1946
Shankweiler's Drive-In Theater, Pennsylvania	Lynn Auto Theatre, Ohio	Saco Drive-In, Maine	Sunset Drive-In Theater, Pennsylvania	Hiway 50 Drive-In Theater, Tennessee

State with the
Oldest Temple

Rhode Island

The Touro Synagogue was dedicated during Hanukkah in December 1763 and is the oldest temple in the United States. Located in Newport, Rhode Island, the temple was designed by famous architect Peter Harrison and took four years to complete. In addition to serving as a symbol of religious freedom, the temple played another part in the country's history. When the British captured Newport in 1776, the temple briefly became a British hospital. Then, in 1781, George Washington met General Lafayette there to plan the final battles of the Revolution.

The United States'
OLDEST TEMPLES

Year opened

1763	1824	1825	1849	1886
Touro Synagogue, Rhode Island	Kahal Kadosh Beth Elohim Synagogue, South Carolina	B'nai Jeshurun, New York	Shul of New York, New York	Oheve Sholom Talmud Torah, District of Columbia

State with the
Oldest Landscaped Gardens

South Carolina

The geometrical garden patterns in Middleton Place Gardens were designed by Henry Middleton in 1741 and were modeled after the gardens at the Palace of Versailles in France. They were first opened to the public in the 1920s. Today, the gardens on this 65-acre (26.3 ha) Charleston plantation are laid out in almost the same fashion as when they were planted more than 250 years ago. Some of the plants that are featured at Middleton Place Gardens include camellia, daffodil, magnolia, jasmine, columbine, and hydrangea. The House Museum is also located on the grounds and displays some of the Middleton family's furniture, art, and documents.

The United States'
OLDEST LANDSCAPED GARDENS

Year established

1741	1853	1891	1907	1932
Middleton Place Gardens, South Carolina	Missouri Botanical Gardens, Missouri	New York Botanical Gardens, New York	Longwood Gardens, Pennsylvania	Hershey Gardens, Pennsylvania

285

State with the Largest
Petrified Wood Collection

South Dakota

Lemmon's Petrified Wood Park in South Dakota is home to 30 acres (12.1 ha) of petrified wood. It covers an entire city block in downtown Lemmon. It was built between 1930 and 1932 when locals collected petrified wood from the area and constructed displays. One structure in the park known as The Castle weighs more than 300 pounds (136 kg) and is made partly from petrified wood and partly of petrified dinosaur and mammoth bones. Other exhibits include a wishing well, a waterfall, the Lemmon Pioneer Museum, and hundreds of pile sculptures.

The United States'
LARGEST PETRIFIED WOOD COLLECTIONS

Area in acres/hectares

30 ac. 12.1 ha.	27 ac. 10.9 ha.	24 ac. 9.7 ha.	20 ac. 8.1 ha.	18 ac. 7.3 ha.
Lemmon's Petrified Wood Park, South Dakota	Long Logs Forest, Arizona	Rainbow Forest, Arizona	Crystal Forest, Arizona	Black Forest, Arizona

State with the World's
Largest Freshwater Aquarium

Tennessee

The Tennessee Aquarium in Chattanooga is an impressive 130,000 square feet (12,077 sq m), making it the largest freshwater aquarium in the world. The $45-million building holds a total of 400,000 gallons (1,514,165 l) of water. In addition, the aquarium features a 60,000-square-foot (5,574-sq-m) building dedicated to the ocean and the creatures that live there. Permanent features in the aquarium include Discovery Hall, and an Environmental Learning Lab. Some of the aquarium's 12,000 animals include baby alligators, paddlefish, lake sturgeon, seadragons, and pipefish. And to feed all of these creatures, the aquarium goes through 12,000 crickets, 33,300 worms, and 1,200 pounds (545 kg) of seafood each month!

The World's
LARGEST FRESHWATER AQUARIUMS

Size in square feet/ square meters

130,000 sq. ft. 12,077 sq. m.	91,494 sq. ft. 8,500 sq. m.	62,382 sq. ft. 5,795 sq. m.	49,514 sq. ft. 4,600 sq. m.	46,284 sq. ft. 4,300 sq. m.
Tennessee Aquarium, Tennessee, USA	The Freshwater Center, Denmark	Great Lakes Aquarium, Minnesota, USA	Aquarium of the Lakes, Britain	Gifu Freshwater Aquarium, Japan

State with the
Biggest Ferris Wheel

Texas

The State Fair of Texas boasts the nation's largest Ferris wheel. Called the Texas Star, this colossal wheel measures 212 feet (64.6 m) high. That's taller than a 20-story building! The Texas Star was built in Italy and shipped to Texas for its debut at the 1986 fair. Located in the 277-acre (112 ha) Fair Park, the Texas Star is just one of the 70 rides featured at the fair. The three-week-long State Fair of Texas is the biggest state fair in the country and brings in about $350 million in revenues annually. It is held in the fall, and the giant Ferris wheel is not the only grand-scale item there. Big Tex, a 52-foot- (15.9-m-) tall cowboy, is the fair's mascot and the biggest cowboy in the United States.

The United States'
FERRIS WHEELS

Height of wheel in feet/meters

212 ft. 64.6 m.	150 ft. 45.8 m.	150 ft. 45.8 m.	150 ft. 45.8 m.	150 ft. 45.8 m.
Texas Star, Texas	Giant Wheel, Ohio	Navy Pier Ferris Wheel, Illinois	Six Flags Ferris Wheel, Kentucky	Wonder Wheel, New York

State with the World's
Largest Human-Made Hole

Utah

Bingham Canyon—a working mine in the Oquirrh Mountains—is the largest human-made hole in the world. It measures 2.5 miles (4 km) wide and 0.75 miles (1.2 km) deep, covering about 1,900 acres (769 ha). It is so large that astronauts can even see it from space. Miners first began digging in the area in 1903. Today approximately 63 million tons (57 million t) of ore and 123 million tons (112 million t) of waste are removed from the canyon each year. Bingham Canyon is one of the largest copper mining operations in the world. It has produced more than 17 million tons (15.4 million t) of copper and 23 million ounces (652 mg) of gold in the last 100 years. Silver is also mined there.

The World's
LARGEST HUMAN-MADE HOLES

Width of opening in miles/kilometers

2.5 mi. 4.0 km.	2.0 mi. 3.2 km.	1.1 mi. 1.8 km.	0.5 mi. 0.8 km.	0.1 mi. 0.16 km.
Bingham Canyon, Utah	Hull-Rust Mahoning Mine, Minnesota	Berkeley Pit, Minnesota	Big Hole Diamond Mine, South Africa	Rublislaw Quarry, Scotland

State That Produces the Most Maple Syrup

Vermont

Maple syrup production in Vermont totaled 460,000 gallons (1,741,000 l) in 2006 and accounted for about 32% of the United States' total yield that year. There are about 2,000 maple syrup producers with 2.17 million tree taps in Vermont, and the annual production generates more than $14 million. It takes about five tree taps to collect enough maple sap—approximately 40 gallons (151.4 l)—to produce just 1 gallon (3.79 l) of syrup. Vermont maple syrup is also made into maple sugar, maple cream, and maple candies.

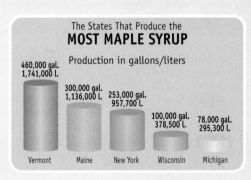

The States That Produce the
MOST MAPLE SYRUP

Production in gallons/liters

460,000 gal.
1,741,000 l.

300,000 gal.
1,136,000 l.

253,000 gal.
957,700 l.

100,000 gal.
378,500 l.

78,000 gal.
295,300 l.

Vermont   Maine   New York   Wisconsin   Michigan

State with the
Largest Office Building

Virginia

The United States'
LARGEST OFFICE BUILDINGS

Size in square feet/square meters

6.63 M sq. ft.
616,000 sq. m.

4.40 M sq. ft.
409,000 sq. m.

2.50 M sq. ft.
232,000 sq. m.

2.10 M sq. ft.
195,000 sq. m.

1.20 M sq. ft.
111,000 sq. m.

| Pentagon, Virginia | Sears Tower, Illinois | Aon Center, Illinois | Empire State Building, New York | Chrysler Building, New York |

The Pentagon Building in Arlington, Virginia, measures 6,636,360 square feet (616,538 sq m) and covers 583 acres (236 ha). In fact, the National Capitol can fit inside the building five times! Although the Pentagon contains 17.5 miles (28.2 km) of hallways, the design of the building allows people to reach any destination in about 7 minutes. The Pentagon is almost like a small city, employing about 23,000 people. About 200,000 phone calls are made there daily, and the internal post office handles about 1.2 million pieces of mail each month.

291

State with the
Longest Train Tunnel

Washington

CASCADE TUNNEL
7.8 MILES LONG   ELEVATION 2247 FEET
41,152 FEET LONG   COMPLETED 1928

The United States'
LONGEST TRAIN TUNNELS

Length miles/kilometers

7.79 mi. 12.6 km.	7.78 mi. 12.5 km.	6.21 mi. 10.0 km.	4.70 mi. 7.56 km.	3.60 mi. 5.79 km.
Cascade Tunnel, Washington	Flathead Tunnel, Missouri	Moffat Tunnel, Colorado	Hoosac Tunnel, Massachusetts	BART Transbay Tube, California

The Cascade Tunnel runs through the Cascade Mountains in central Washington and measures almost 7.8 miles (12.6 km) long. The tunnel connects the towns of Berne and Scenic. It was built by the Great Northern Railway in 1929 to replace the original tunnel that was built at an elevation frequently hit with snow slides. To help cool the trains' diesel engines and remove fumes, the tunnel is equipped with huge fans that blow air during and after a train pass.

State with the Country's
Oldest Spa

West Virginia

GEORGE WASHINGTON'S
BATH TUB (1748)

The town of Bath in West Virginia is home to the country's first spa. In 1776, George Washington incorporated the town and named it Bath after the famous English town known for its Roman baths. Washington and his family relaxed in the healing waters, and eventually built a house nearby the increasingly popular health resort. Located in West Virginia's eastern panhandle, the Warm Spring Ridge produces about 2,000 gallons of water per minute at a temperature of 74°F. Today people come to Bath, which is also known as Berkeley Springs, for relaxation and health treatments.

The United States'
OLDEST SPAS

By year of incorporation

1776	1844	1854	1880	1909
Berkeley Springs, West Virginia	Warmer Springs Ranch, California	Vichy Hot Springs, California	Ojo Caliente, New Mexico	Steamboat Villa Hot Springs, Nevada

State with the Country's Largest Water Park

Wisconsin

Noah's Ark in Wisconsin Dells sprawls for 70 acres (28.4 ha) and includes 36 waterslides. One of the most popular—Dark Voyage—takes visitors on a twisting rapids ride in the dark. The ride can pump 8,000 gallons (30,283 l) of water a minute. Visitors can also enjoy two wave pools, two mile-long "endless" rivers, and four children's play areas. It takes 5 million gallons (19 million l) of water—the equivalent of more than 14 Olympic swimming pools—to fill all the pools and operate the 3 miles (4.8 km) of waterslides.

In 2006, the park's Time Warp ride opened. It's the world's largest family barrel ride, which twists riders down a 70-foot (21 m) hill at 30 miles (48 km) per hour.

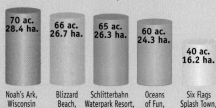

The United States'
LARGEST WATER PARKS

Size in acres/hectares

70 ac. 28.4 ha.	66 ac. 26.7 ha.	65 ac. 26.3 ha.	60 ac. 24.3 ha.	40 ac. 16.2 ha.
Noah's Ark, Wisconsin	Blizzard Beach, Florida	Schlitterbahn Waterpark Resort, Texas	Oceans of Fun, Missouri	Six Flags Splash Town, Texas

State with the
Largest Coal Mine

Wyoming

Black Thunder Mine is located near Wright, Wyoming, and produces about 87.6 million tons (79.5 million t) of coal each year. That's about 10% of the country's total production. The mine uses a giant earth-scraping machine that can extract about 3 tons (2.7 t) of coal per second! Miners fill about 25 miles (40 km) of coal cars each day. Black Thunder—which opened in 1977—has approximately 1 billion tons (907 million t) of coal still in the mine. Black Thunder is owned by Arch Coal—one of the world's largest coal producers—and employs about 600 people.

The United States'
LARGEST COAL MINES

Coal produced annually, in tons and metric tons

Black Thunder, Wyoming	North Antelope Rochelle, Wyoming	MIBRAG, Missouri	Freedom Mine, North Dakota	Bailey Mine, Pennsylvania
87.6 M tons 79.5 M t.	82.7 M tons 75.0 M t.	18.0 M tons 16.3 M t.	16.2 M tons 14.7 M t.	11.1 M tons 10.1 t.

INDEX

● ● ● ● ● ● ● ●

WILD WACKY AND AMAZING FACTS

Movies · Television
Food · Sports · Animals
Music · Holidays

Happy Valentine

TASTE-IN

State of the Plate

Fillmore, the VW autobus in *Cars the Movie*, had the license plate 51237. This was done to celebrate the birthday of George Carlin—the voice of Fillmore—which is May 12, 1937. Oddly enough, it also turned out to be the zip code of George, Iowa.

The Kent Family farm in the new *Superman* movie was originally built on a soundstage in Sydney, Australia—the location of the rest of the film. However, it did not look very authentic, so the set was scrapped and the crew flew to another part of the country to create a real farm. Workers constructed 4.5 miles (7 km) of road and planted 30 acres (12 ha) of corn. It took more than three months for the corn to grow tall enough, and it was very hard to maintain because Australia was at the end of a seven-year drought.

Filming the Farm

Penguin Pizzazz

All those dancing penguins in the movie *Happy Feet* look so authentic because they are based on the movements of actual dancers wearing motion capture sensor suits. This even included special head gear equipped with beaks so the dancers' moves were more authentic. The dancers also had to complete "penguin school" before performing to become familiar with the birds' movements.

The set crew had to get pretty creative while filming the fair scenes in *Charlotte's Web*. Directors worried that the film's extras would get motion sickness on the fair rides as they filmed very long days for more than a week. So the art department made casts from their own faces and secured them to dummies that rode the rides without complaint. And since the filming was done in summer, instead of in autumn as was the time in the movie, they also had to spray paint all of the trees orange and yellow.

More Than Meets the Eye

Pet Perspective

Most of the scenes from the movie *Over the Hedge* are shown from the animals' perspective. To get an idea of how these scenes should be drawn, one animator working on the film strapped a mini video camera to a friend's dog and let him run around the house for a while. The footage he collected clued illustrators in to what animals actually see so close to the ground.

Character Continuation

Richard Belzer, who plays Detective John Munch on *Law & Order: Special Victims Unit*, holds the record for playing the same character on the most television shows. He first appeared as Detective Munch on *Homicide: Life on the Streets* in 1993. This led to several crossovers, including *Law & Order*, *The X-Files*, *The Beat*, *Law & Order: Trial By Jury*, and the finale of *Arrested Development*.

Is There a Doctor in the House?

The set of *Desperate Housewives* seems a bit unlucky for the leading ladies. In 2004, Eva Longoria, who plays Gabrielle, was briefly knocked unconscious when a pole on the set hit her in the head. Later that year, Terri Hatcher broke two ribs when she tripped over a wedding cake prop. The following year, Hatcher was again injured on the set when a lightbulb exploded near her face. Luckily, both Housewives fully recovered.

Product Placement

American Idol leads all other TV shows in product placement with 4,085 occurrences in one season. That means that the show flashed brand-name products 4,085 times without being considered commercials. This is even more surprising considering *American Idol* runs only from January to May. The two most frequently displayed products are Coca-Cola and Cingular Wireless.

On the game show *Deal or No Deal*, all of the money in the twenty-six briefcases totals $3,418,416.01. The smallest cash prize is 1 cent, and the largest cash prize is $1 million. To date, the largest prize won on the show from a briefcase was $750,000.

Dealing in Dough

Did Someone Say Jetlag?

The contestants on *The Amazing Race: All Stars* will travel more than 45,000 miles (72,421 km) and visit 5 continents in just 28 days. That's an average of 1,607 miles (2,586 km) a day—or the distance from New York to Texas. The final three teams took more than 25 different flights and journeyed thousands of miles by bus, train, taxi, and car, all in hopes of winning the $1 million grand prize.

Each winter, Walt Disney World creates dozens of delicious life-sized decorations. At the Grand Floridian Resort, a gigantic gift shop made completely of gingerbread takes 400 hours to bake and 160 hours to decorate. The Beach Club Resort features a huge carousel made of sugar paste, chocolate, and gingerbread. Some of the ingredients used to create this edible masterpiece include 96 pounds (44 kg) of flour, 100 pounds (45 kg) of icing, 36 pounds (16 kg) of honey, and 50 pounds (23 kg) of dark chocolate.

Gigantic Gingerbread

Gobs of Gum

Kids in North America spend about $500 million on bubble gum every year. This equals about 40 million pieces every day, some 1.6 million pieces every hour, and 26,000 every minute or 444 pieces per second. The most popular flavors are cinnamon, spearmint, and peppermint.

Food

Shoveling It In

The average American eats almost 1,500 pounds (680 kg) of food each year. Some of the foods that make up this total include 150 pounds (68 kg) of meat, 290 pounds (132 kg) of milk and cream, 35 pounds (16 kg) of eggs, 48 pounds (22 kg) of chicken, 68 pounds (31 kg) of bread, 125 pounds (57 kg) of potatoes, and 80 pounds (36 kg) of fruit.

One Cool Cookie

Thin Mints are the most popular flavor of Girl Scout cookies, accounting for about 19% of total sales each year. Thin Mints are produced at a rate of almost 2 million per day in an oven that measures more than 300 feet (91 m) long. Once the cookie is baked, it must travel 300 feet (91 m) on a conveyor belt to cool before being coated with chocolate. Thin Mints have been sold by the Girl Scouts since 1951.

Americans buy about 90 million pounds of marshmallows each year—about the same weight as 1,300 gray whales! Marshmallow sales total about $125 million annually, and are highest in summer. During this season, about half of all marshmallows sold are toasted over fire. The marshmallow capital of the world is located in Ligonier, Indiana, which holds a giant festival each year celebrating the toasty treat.

Toasty Treats

Kickin' Kid

Freddy Adu became the youngest professional athlete in recent history when he signed with the Major League Soccer team DC United when he was just 14 years old. He didn't play much during his first season, but he has recently become one of the most impressive players in the league.

The Tall and Short of It

The tallest men ever to play in the NBA are Gheorghe Muresan and Manute Bol—both measuring 7 feet, 7 inches (2.3 m) tall. Muresan played from 1993 to 2000 and Bol played from 1985 to 1995. The shortest person to play in the NBA was Tyrone "Muggsy" Bogues, and he measured 5 feet, 3 inches (1.6 m). Bogues played from 1987 to 2001. If he ever played against Muresan or Bol, Bogues would be almost 2.5 feet (0.8 m) below them!

Kudos to the Cards

After the St. Louis Cardinals won the World Series in 2006, they became the most-winning team in the National League with 10 victories. The Cardinals have played in 17 World Series Championships since 1926. During the 2006 season, the Cardinals played 161 games and won 83 of them. Throughout the year, more than 3.4 million fans packed the stadium.

Patching Up Players

Football players aren't the only people seeing action during a game. Each NFL team has two or three athletic trainers collectively performing more than 5,000 medical treatments each season. The training staff uses about 71 miles (114 km) of athletic tape per year. That's enough tape to stretch across the entire length of a football field 1,041 times.

The Stanley Cup isn't just for hockey games anymore. In 2003, winning New Jersey Devils goaltender Martin Brodeur took the cup to a movie theater and ate popcorn out of it. In 1996, Colorado Avalanche player Sylvain Lefebvre had his first child baptized in it.

Creative Cup

Speak Up!

A lion's roar can be heard for more than 5 miles (8 km)! Lions are most likely to roar after sunset. Besides roaring to intimidate other animals, lions use their call to let the others in their pride know where they are. Females also roar to call their cubs.

Sailing Snakes

Snakes can't really fly like birds do, but certain species in the rain forests of Southeast Asia can move from treetop to treetop with the greatest of ease. These snakes flatten themselves out by sucking their guts and forming a U-shape. By twisting back and forth, these three-foot (1 m) snakes can cover more feet 330 feet (100 m) at one time.

Undercover Octopus

The mimic octopus is a true master of disguise. It can contort its body to resemble the shape and color of dangerous sea creatures to fool its predators. Some of the deadly creatures it often mimics include lionfish, sea snakes, and mantis shrimp.

The hagfish is a bottom-dwelling creature that can release a slime that surrounds its body when it is attacked. The slime is so thick that it can suffocate the predator. But, if the hagfish isn't careful, it can also suffocate in its own slime. When the hagfish feels safe again, it knots up its body to squeeze out the excess slime.

Sea of Slime

When the first rains of the wet season begin on Christmas Island off the coast of Australia, residents will soon be seeing red. At this time, some 120 million crabs seem to pop out of everywhere and race toward the sea. They travel across jungles, down cliffs, across roads, and sometimes into houses. This red blanket of crustaceans can move at speeds of 300 feet (91 m) per hour.

Crabby Commuting

1

Moon Man Memento

The MTV Music Awards gives out silver trophies shaped like astronauts holding MTV flags and are called Moon Men. Peter Gabriel holds the record for the most awards in one night for the *Sledgehammer* video. Madonna holds the record for the most total awards with 21 Moon Men.

Radio Roundup

According to Nielsen BDS and Arbitron—two companies that study radio airplay across the country—the most played song of 2006 was Mary J. Blige's "Be Without You." The songs that round out the top five include Sean Paul's "Temperature," Cassie's "Me & U," Shakira's "Hips Don't Lie," and Natasha Bedingfield's "Unwritten."

Salute to Songs

Each year, the Recording Academy inducts songs into the Grammy Hall of Fame. In 2007, they added 44 songs, bringing the total songs honored to 728. Some of the latest entries include Van Morrison's "Brown-Eyed Girl," Spike Jones's "All I Want for Christmas (Is My Two Front Teeth)," and "*Star Wars*— Motion Picture Soundtrack."

During the first week of 2007, The *Dreamgirls* soundtrack was the bestselling album in the United States. However, it was the worst-selling number one in Soundscan history with 66,000 copies sold. Soundscan tracks music sales throughout North America each week and provides the data for the Billboard Charts. Part of the soundtrack's low numbers for the week can be explained by the fact that music downloads outsold albums more than two to one that week.

The Bottom of the Top

Downloads Are Up

Single-track music downloads went through the roof in 2006, with nearly 795 million songs downloaded. That's an 89% increase from the previous year. The United States accounts for the most downloads with 582 million, followed by the UK with 53 million downloads.

Most malls have decorated for the winter holidays by November 1, and the most frequently played songs are "Jingle Bells" and "White Christmas." The busiest shopping day at malls is the Saturday before Christmas. About 70% of malls offer gift-wrapping services, with each mall covering about 4,150 presents during the season. Each mall Santa will be visited by about 7,720 children—an average of 257 a day—between Thanksgiving and Christmas.

Christmas Crunch

Scare Up Some Profits

About 82% of all kids in the United States take part in Halloween, as well as about 67% of adults. Americans spend about $1.5 billion on costumes annually; more than $2.5 billion on Halloween decorations, cards, and crafts; and almost $2 billion on candy. Not surprisingly, Halloween is the second most profitable holiday behind Christmas.